For Lindsey
A lovely surprise in the midst of it all

ACKNOWLEDGEMENTS

Athletes need backboards off which to bounce balls, trainers to soothe aching muscles, coaches to enhance their technical skills, and other players with whom to practice. Writers' needs are little different. Carol Hallenbeck and I have batted ideas back and forth for years; my husband Dave patiently supports and encourages me; Carol and Dick Schwartz have been thorough editors; and numerous audiences of adoptors, pre-adoptors, and professionals have provided the feedback that has honed this book's message. My thanks to all, and to my children, who have grown up listening to a pecking typewriter and a whirring computer.

Pat Johnston
September, 1984

AN ADOPTOR'S ADVOCATE

by

Patricia Irwin Johnston

Perspectives Press / Fort Wayne

Perspectives Press
905 West Wildwood Avenue
Fort Wayne, Indiana 46807

Manufactured in the United States of America.

First Printing, November, 1984
Second Printing, December, 1985

The author gratefully acknowledges the following:

Victoria Andres, *"Not Really Yours."* Used by permission.
Marilee Richards, *"The Intake Interview."*
   Used by permission.
E. Van Clef, *"Lullaby for an Adopted Child."*
   Used by permission.
E. Van Clef, *"Burial."* Used by permission.

LIBRARY OF CONGRESS CATALOGING IN PUBLICATION DATA

Johnston, Patricia Irwin.
   An adoptor's advocate.

   Bibliography: p. 96
   Includes index.
   1. Adoption—United States.   2. Childlessness—United States—Psychological aspects.   3. Foster parents—United States—Psychology.   4. Social workers—United States.
I. Title.
HV875.55.J64 1984   362.7'34'0973   84-22702
ISBN 0-9609504-2-7

TABLE OF CONTENTS

CHAPTER 1

THE LETTER

The face of adoption is changing in late twentieth century America. Every year hundreds of social service agencies across the country drop their adoption programs or go out of business entirely; fewer and fewer young women dealing with untimely pregnancies approach placement agencies for services; and more and more children who are older, handicapped or part of sibling groups find their way into the adoption resource books. The majority of potential adoptors, however, still fit the traditional mold: they are infertile couples adopting because they cannot conceive children biologically related to them both, and most of them seek to adopt healthy infants. Whereas twenty years ago the traditional adoptor would also have limited his choice of a child to an infant of his own race or ethnic background, increasingly traditional adoptors are considering the adoption of biracial American infants or adopting from foreign countries.

Some people attribute these changes in the adoption system to a shortage of adoptable babies brought about by contraception and by societal pressures that have resulted in large numbers of women experiencing problem pregnancies choosing to parent their children themselves. To a certain extent this is true, but it doesn't explain all of the changes. There are still thousands of infants for whom adoption plans are made each year — at least half of them privately placed without the assistance of agencies.

Why are the traditional clients of child placement agencies no longer seeking their services? Because agencies are in many cases unresponsive to their needs.

This book was born of the frustration felt by dozens and dozens of couples with whom I've worked and from whom I've heard in several years as an adoption and infertility advocate. It has a special focus: not infertility in general or adoption in general, but infertility and adoption together. I will leave it to others to address the unanswered needs of birthparents and adoptees. My dual audience is made up of traditional adoptors and the professionals who work with them. The book's purposes are to correct some misunderstandings about infertility and traditional adoption, to bring out into the open some of those most carefully concealed fears and doubts that preadoptive parents experience, to help couples and counselors understand the emotional processes that connect infertility and adoption, and to offer some suggestions for improving the system for the benefit of all concerned. What makes this focus important is that traditional adoptors still form the largest pool of potential adoptors for the waiting children who now are adoption agencies' primary clients. It is vital, then, that social service professionals be understanding of and responsive to the needs of such couples if ever they are to work with them in ways that both can term productive.

The letter below is a real one, actually mailed in a slightly longer and more detailed version by a family of three to an agency with whom they had "worked" for several years.

Dear Caseworker,

How perfectly furious it makes us that we do not have control of our own lives! **Most** couples decide for themselves when the time is right for a baby. **Most** couples need not ask for references from their parents, friends, neighbors, employers or clergymen before planning additions to their families. **Most** couples have health insurance that helps to cover the financial strain of the arrival of a new child. **Most** couples decide on their own whether or not both of their children's parents should work outside the home. **Most** couples do not live each day of their lives over a span of several years of family planning with the anxious knowledge that any time, any day, the phone might ring, and, with no warning, no precise nine month wait, no gradual acquisition of correctly sized clothes and appropriate toys, no previous guarantees that carefully made vacation plans or education or job commitments could be carried out, a caller may say, "Are you ready? There is a one day/three month/one year old boy/girl waiting to be yours if you say the word."

But we aren't **most** couples. We are an infertile couple. Frankly, we came to adoption as a second choice, our primary motivation a selfish one — we wanted a baby and we couldn't make one. But this wasn't something we felt that we could openly share with you. Nor could we share with you how humiliating it felt to need to prove ourselves to you and to those whom we had to ask to fill out reference forms for us before we could have a child placed in our home. Though in our private conversations with each other we talked about what financial strategies we would need to follow in order to save enough money to "buy" our baby from you, we feared that you would be horrified and insulted if we shared with you our feeling that the fee you needed to charge us was a purchase price. We got all kinds of messages from both you and from society in general about the process we were entering, and because those messages were so mixed, we felt it safer to say nothing, even when we felt strongly about something you were saying or doing. Because we acknowledged your expertise and questioned our own, we smiled and nodded and agreed to whatever you asked of us without daring to question anything in your agency's process of adoption.

Surprised at the depth of our own reactions to our thwarted family plans, we found it difficult to trust that anyone could truly understand us and the trauma to an individual or to a relationship that comes of being found to be infertile and considering the alternative of adoption. The only way this can truly be grasped is to be infertile oneself and to want children. How we'd love to insist that all caseworkers be adoptive parents, but we know that this is both impractical and impossible.

Though in most other aspects of our lives we are assertive people, we didn't dare assert ourselves with you, Dear Caseworker. You were too powerful. With you rested our only hope of being parents.

But now that we are parents, Dear Caseworker, we need to speak, because the system we dealt with, an old and beleagured system entrenched in tradition rather than responsive to changing needs, needs revision. As it is it hurts too much, and, having satisfied our desire for a baby, even realizing that there are other, older children out there who need us, we can't quite bring ourselves to risk again the adoption system's humiliating pain. Fix it, Dear Caseworker. It shouldn't have to be this way.

An Adoptive Couple

This letter, obviously written in great pain and at what the writer felt was some risk, was not responded to. Amazing, you say, that a social service agency would not have responded to a consumer's plea for sensitivity? Amazing, perhaps, but no uncommon. Was the caseworker insensitive? Absolutely not! She was simply too busy to respond. But because there was no response, this family, like thousands of others who make the same decision every day, voluntarily chose not to further expand their family by adopting one of the several thousand waiting children whose very existence makes this caseworker's job so difficult, because the institutionalized adoption process and its system are simply too difficult and too painful to subject themselves to repeatedly. In light of the fact that a recent study indicated that over 50% of couples both fertile and infertile would consider adoption in expanding their families, this failure to communicate effectively is particularly sad. [1]

In fact, the adoption system as it is is burning out not just the professionals working within in, but the pool of families who might potentially adopt the children who wait. It is a system in need of vast changes.

---

1. Feigelman, William and Arnold R. Silverman, *Chosen Children: New Patterns of Adoptive Relationships.* New York: Praeger, 1983, p. 13.

CHAPTER 2

THE CASEWORKER AND THE TRADITIONAL ADOPTOR

The Intake Interview
by Marilee Richards

A closet size interviewing room, windowless
and gray. A middle-aged couple steps in and
sits down. They both look at me, silent,
expectant, hopeful.
They want a baby.
The room is warm. Little beads of sweat are
forming on the man's forehead. He would like
to comfort his wife. After a minute he puts his hand
over hers in her lap.

The fluorescent lamps buzz softly to themselves
and pulse down a blue light that turns
the woman's lipstick purple
and makes us all feel old.

The woman is slight and looks even smaller
as she shrinks in toward her husband.
She begins to shred a Kleenex with her fingers.
The ghost of her unconceived child
stares out at me from behind her eyes.

They have waited to see me for over two years.
I feel weary for these people, I know
their story already. Still, we move through
the desperate routine like
three haggard dancers.

They have been doing biological gymnastics
for seven years. The woman
has taken her temperature every morning
for three years
The man has masturbated
in the doctor's stainless steel bathroom
and then waited
while a technician examined his semen
under a microscope. The numbers seemed adequate
but the sperm weren't very wiggly.

One morning the couple
stayed home from work and made love
at exactly nine o'clock and then
rushed to the doctor so he could
do something to the woman's cervix while
she lay on her back on his
examination table . . . Several times
the doctor even squirted some of the husband's
sperm into her cervix with a plastic syringe,
mixed with the more athletic sperm
of a young medical student
so if the woman ever did have a baby
the man could think that it might be his.

Recently they have stopped making love
altogether.

They unravel the most private threads
of their lives to me, quivering
with the importance of this hour.
It is almost noon. I am hungry.
I am thinking that I know enough
of these people. I am ashamed

at not having more feeling for them.
An infantryman, after shooting a hole
through his fiftieth or two hundredth enemy,
must have similar thoughts. No wonder
soldiers are all crazy when they come home.

The room seems warmer.
The man unbuttons his jacket.
They now offer their professional jobs,
their cultured hobbies,
their gardened surburban home.
"Just look," they are saying,
"See how worthy we are, how deserving."
"See how long we have waited."
"Look," I say back (in so many words)
"I would give you a dozen babies
if I could."

But I have little to offer.
There are no babies now.
I tell them. The babies are all on the Pill,
or sucked out of their cozy wombs
in the tenth week of fetal life.
A few are alive and well and living
with their thirteen year old mothers.

The man and woman eye me suspiciously,
certain that I have a desk drawer full
of babies in my office who I
hand out like lollipops to other people,
the couple whom I saw yesterday
and will see tomorrow.

I tell them that I will see
them again in another year. We will have
some more interviews.
They will fill out some more forms.
Maybe there will be a baby for them then.

The man's hair recedes a little further.
The woman feels another line sink
into her forehead. For a moment
they are silent, staring past me at
patterns on the wall.

When they leave
the door clangs behind them
like an echo in a cavern.

Adoption workers are threatening. No matter how un-threatening the caseworker feels, no matter how kind, understanding, knowledgeable, and compassionate s/he is, s/he is still perceived as a threat by nearly every client— fertile of infertile— who walks through the office door for the purpose of inquiring about adoption, whether it be for the adoption of a healthy baby or the adoption of a handicapped biracial teenager.

Control is the issue that makes this so. In modern society a feeling of being in control of one's destiny is vital to a sense of well being. Losing control through illness, accident or uncontrollable circumstances is very difficult. Even people who consider themselves to be very religious may have difficulty turning over control of their destiny to a supreme being. Yet this is what the concept of religious faith demands.

To be asked to turn over to another human being complete control of an area of their lives which most people take very much for granted —family planning —is particularly hard for preadoptive parents. Yet this is precisely what adoption demands.

No one licenses parents. There are controls on marriage and divorce that require societal intervention to do or to undo. We must meet certain requirements to complete education, to drive a car, to obtain a job, to qualify to vote, to buy property, but if one is biologically able to reproduce one is not required to qualify to become a parent. Our laws and social customs assume that the biological relationship between progenitor and offspring is inherently inviolable except under the most dire of circumstances, that society generally has no business interfering in the parent/child relationship.

When adoption is looked at from the point of view of the would-be parent, who is asked to defend personal values, plans, goals, motivations, relationships, finances under examination by one who has the absolute power to grant parenthood (whether of a first child or of a fifteenth), perhaps it isn't too difficult to understand why preadoptive parents find it hard to relinquish this control.

Who is this person? many ask themselves. What qualifications, educational or personal, equip him or her to hold these God-like powers? Since most parents aren't evaluated and licensed, how will our suitability be determined? Where are the written criteria for what constitutes parental fitness, and if such criteria are not written, what qualifies this person (perhaps young and/or unmarried and/or not a parent or at least almost never an adoptive parent) to determine whether or not we are parent material? If we are approved, what qualifies this person to decide which child, how young or how old, what sex or color, how healthy or unhealthy, we are qualified to parent?

All preadoptive parents ask these questions silently, but very few openly question the social worker. To other adoptive parents, such questions seem perfectly logical; to some adoption workers such questions seem insulting and even threatening. I am a professional, such workers say, qualified by training and study to do such work. Would you, they ask, seek only a diabetic doctor to treat you for diabetes? No! You would choose your doctor on the basis of his educational qualifications and trust his knowledge. If you didn't trust him you would change doctors. The same, then, should be true of your relationship with me.

In the crux of this argument —that one places trust in a professional by virtue of his education and thus his expertise and that in the absence of this trust one finds a new professional —lies the heart of the problem as perceived by many potential adoptors. Adoption is a difficult and slow process. Potential adoptors do not feel that they have the power to pick and choose their agencies as they would a doctor because there are fewer and fewer agencies processing adoptions, and because there are restrictions on age, religion, length of marriage, etc., they do not qualify at all agencies. They may not feel that they have the power to pick and choose social workers within an agency because many agencies don't have a large number of adoption workers. As well, unlike the situation of a patient electing to see a doctor who practices in a group, where the patient is allowed to

decide with which physician he wishes to make an appoint-
ment, at an adoption agency couples are randomly assigned
to a worker and then may fear that a request for a change in
worker may be negatively received and thus cause them to
risk general disapproval by the agency.

Would-be parents _feel_ powerless. The degree of powerlessness they feel is in many cases directly proportional to
their perceived need to adopt. The infertile couple or the
single person with no children at all and with a deep desire to
parent may feel most powerless. The couple with four biological children who have also adopted six times and are
being asked to consider a sibling group may feel least
powerless. Yet all of them probably do feel or have in the past
felt the frustration of losing control to a social worker.

Traditional adoptors also feel vulnerable. Unlike preferential adoptors, who come to adoption with the biological
capability of expanding their families as a kind of insurance
should the adoption not work out, infertile couples know that
adoption may be their last chance for parenthood. Because
society does perceive adoption as a second best alternative
for them, they may, too, and it may have taken a great deal of
careful introspection as they went through the grief process
for the biological child of their assumptions for them to have
been able to feel positively about this compromise to their
original life plans. But adoption is changing, and they may be
asked to make more and more compromises if they are to
parent.

There is no way for adoption workers to completely erase
the adversarial relationship that traditional adoptors may
feel toward them. This perception is part of the situation, and
much of that can't be changed. There are ways, though, for
caseworkers to ease this tension. Primarily they involve the
professionals first accepting that they may be expecting too
much from themselves in thinking that they alone can
adequately prepare an adoptor for parenting. In seeing
oneself not as the grantor of children but as the preparer of
parents, a professional becomes himself an adoptor's advocate. If professionals truly see themselves in this role, they

will work toward more flexibility and humanness in the system, more responsiveness in and justification for policy, better training of social workers and foster parents, less theory and more practicality in parent preparation, better communication with and referral to other helping professionals and adoption-related services. Adoption professionals have always correctly seen their primary client as the child in need of parents. But only in forming a positive relationship with those parents can they protect the child's best interests.

CHAPTER 3

INFERTILITY HURTS

Burial
by
E. Van Clef

Today I closed the door of the nursery
I have kept for you in my heart.

I can no longer stand in its doorway.
I have waited for you there so long.
I cannot forever live on the periphery
    of the dream world we share, and you
    cannot enter my world.

I have fought to bring you across the
    threshold of conception and birth.
I have fought time, doctors, devils and
    God Almighty.
I am weary and there is no victory.

Other children may someday live in my
    heart but never in your place.

I can never hold you. I can never really
    let you go. But I must go on.
The unborn are forever trapped within the
    living but it is unseemly for the
    living to be trapped forever by the
    unborn.

Successful adoptive parenting, write Jerome Smith and
Franklin I. Miroff in their book *You're Our Child: A Social/
Psychological Approach To Adoption,* is dependent upon a
family successfully engaging in the process of building what
they call a sense of **entitlement** —a true feeling of belong-
ing, parent to child, child to parent. Developing a sense of

entitlement is an ongoing process of growth rather than a single task indentifiably completable, and the success of an adoption is related to the degree to which this sense of entitlement has been acquired by each family member rather than to its being seen as achieved or not achieved. Entitlement, say Smith and Miroff, requires the accomplishment of a series of subtasks which are unique to adoption:

1. Learning to recognize and deal with the psychological ramifications of their own infertility.

2. Coming to recognize that adoptive parenting is different from biological parenting in a number of significant and unavoidable ways.

3. Learning to handle the questions and comments of outsiders or extended family members which often reflect society's general feeling that adoption is a second best alternative for all involved.[1]

Not all adoptive parents are infertile, of course. In their book Chosen Children, Feigelman and Silverman have identified adoptors using two terms: **traditional adoptors,** those who adopt because of infertility or a medical condition that discourages them from reproducing, and **preferential adoptors,** those whose motivations are based on feelings of altruism or social and humanitarian commitment.[2]   This being true, it is apparent that preferential adoptors would not need to work on what Smith and Miroff define as entitlement building's first task, resolving their personal infertility issues. Preferential adoptors do have a related task to accomplish, however: coming to understand and accept their motivations for adoption and to face the practical realism that will come if they follow through with their idealistic interests. This book's focus is the traditional adoptor within the system. So it is the task of resolving infertility issues that we will first examine.
   Resolution of infertility is a task so complicated in itself that

there are over fifty chapters of RESOLVE and several similar groups across the country that have been trying to define it for some time. The process of resolution is an emotional goal aimed for by infertile couples whose initial physical goal was a successfully shared pregnancy. It does not come automatically with a birth or an adoption as so many would like to believe . . . and therein lies the problem. Resolution is a process, too, like entitlement, and for many it is a life long process.

Infertility is on the increase. There are a number of reasons for this, including the tendency for couples today to postpone their family building until their naturally less fertile thirties, an increase in exposure to environmental pollutants and workplace chemicals, an increase in the use of prescription and recreational drugs, and the rampant epidemic of sexually transmitted diseases. Statistically about 30% of couples with a fertility impairment have medical problems which are exclusively the male's, another 30% have exclusively female medical problems, 35% more have combined problems, and about 5% of couples have problems currently undiagnosable. Currently there are over 10,000,000 people of child bearing age in the United States who either cannot conceive at all or who cannot carry a pregnancy to a live birth. They represent nearly one in five couples of child-bearing age.

There has never been a better time nor a worse time to be infertile than now, in the 1980's, in America. On the one hand, things have never looked so promising for a couple just beginning to seek medical help. Until the early 1970's medical expertise could produce a cure for 30% or fewer of couples who were fertility impaired. When RESOLVE was founded in 1973, on the kitchen table of Barbara Eck Menning, a Boston area nurse/midwife, herself infertile, its client base was quite different from today's client base. Infertility was then a closet issue, not discussed openly, sometimes not even acknowledged, because it was perceived as too sexual and was therefore embarrassing. Infertile couples then routinely spent several years in a fertility study, and being seen by a reproductive endocrinologist or a urologist with a special interest in infertility was highly uncommon. The most accurate term to describe the medical condition these couples faced was **infertility** —and for most of them it would be permanent. The major purpose at that time for infertility-oriented groups was to offer support to a couple's grieving over permanent sterility, to guide them to information on alternatives, and to assist them in deciding to adopt, to accept childlessness or to use donor insemination.

Barbara Eck Menning and her Boston members, however, became quite vocal about infertility and demanded that it be seen as a legitimate medical problem with emotional consequences rather than emotional causes. Barbara wrote *Infertility: A Guide For The Childless Couple*. Chapters of RESOLVE and similar smaller groups began to spring up across the country. Their members sought not just support from one another, but advocacy as well. What they were reticent about saying all alone, the group could say for all of them. This vocalness on the part of infertility patients has been in part responsible for a burgeoning in research and a magnification of infertility awareness.

Because of their assertive and productive educational campaigns, infertility-oriented groups such as RESOLVE found that their client base shifted dramatically in just five years. Where once contact was made primarily by couples who had either been given a final diagnosis of absolute sterility or had spent so much time in an unproductive study that they were presuming failure, soon a majority of couples contacted such groups early in the process of acknowledging a fertility problem, were efficiently referred to medical care, became pregnant relatively quickly (as compared to infertility patients of ten years before) and moved on.

Today more appropriate terminology for the medical condition these people experience is **impaired fertility**, a positive term reflecting the fact that 70% of those couples who are unable to conceive after a year of unprotected intercourse or who have been unable to carry a pregnancy to term can now, with appropriate medical care, become biological parents together. Infertility-oriented groups still offer support, but their education and advocacy services are even more frequently used than are support services.

On the other hand, for couples who face the necessity of ceasing to see themselves as fertility impaired and to accept that they are infertile . . . sterile . . . barren . . . things have never looked worse. The new medical successes are more limited to female than to male infertility problems. Additionally, for the thirty percent who will eventually need to accept the permanence of their infertility, the fact that such a high percentage of couples can become pregnant exerts more pressure than ever before to continue trying just one more cycle or just one more treatment. With new breakthroughs being announced daily and a variety of almost science-fiction-like options available or on the horizon, the pressure to keep trying with the assumption that a pregnancy will eventually occur has never been more intense for infertile couples.

Infertile couples today have grown up within the first generation for whom fertility seemed totally controllable. Birth control techniques have been refined in the last twenty years to such an extend that they seem to ensure that those who are not ready to parent need not do so if they are willing to be diligent in practicing a method of birth control.

Society encourages the deliberate planning of lives to include education, training, and the careful establishment of careers with financial security before parenthood is contemplated. We are encouraged to eat healthfully, to be active and fit. For most couples parenthood no longer happens by chance. Instead, a great deal of decision making precedes the attempts of most couples to conceive. Thus, many couples spend large parts of their potentialy most fertile years trying diligently not to get pregnant, never suspecting that in this day of good health and controllable fertility they might find themselves to be infertile when and if they do decide to have a baby.

Think about this anecdote for a moment:

You arrive at the door, arms laden with packages. Inserting the key, you hear your telephone ringing, so you drop keys and scatter packages as you dash to the phone. Just as you pick up the receiver and call out "Hello?" . . . the caller hangs up.

With a mixture of **surprise** and **denial** you think, "Oh, no! I couldn't have missed it!" and you follow up with **anger** at yourself or the caller. ("Darn, why didn't I get there sooner." or "Gosh, they only let it ring three times.")

"If only I hadn't had those packages . . ." comes the magical thinking of **bargaining**. "I really wanted that call," you think as you experience **depression**. Finally you **accept** the loss of the call, thinking, "Oh, well, if it was important they'll call back."

You have experienced a loss, and, depending upon how you typically resolve losses, you may go on with what you were doing and put your packages away, you may substitute for the lost call by phoning a friend, or you may buy an answering machine to prevent missing more calls. Though the process in this case has taken less than a minute, experiencing the full spectrum of loss —**surprise, denial, anger, bargaining, depression, acceptance** —has allowed you to adjust so that you may comfortably move on. [3]

Life is a blend of gains and losses. Daily we experience small losses like the phone call which pass almost unnoticed because we are so accustomed to dealing with them. Every so often, though, life deals us a heavier blow. We find ourselves at a turning point . . . a crossroads. . . a passage. . . embroiled in one of those crucial periods of vulnerability and heightened potential that the psychologist calls a life crisis. In ancient Chinese symbol-writing the symbol for the concept of crisis is a combination of two other symbols: those representing danger and opportunity. While going through a major turning point in our lives we experience repeated danger and opportunity, resulting in failures and achievements, and after each crisis we find ourselves and our lives permanently restructured. Each passage requires us to give up a familiarly comfortable sense of ourselves —some bit of long-held magic —to allow for inner growth. Turning points are never easy, even when they occur because some presumably easy to overcome blockage has occurred in our lives. [4]

Such a turning point is a fertility impairment; and for many people it comes so early in life that it becomes the first life crisis they have faced which seems likely to produce major loss. Infertility undermines an assumption held since childhood: that someday, if and when we want to, we will parent a child conceived in the love we feel for another person who is our life's partner. Facing the possibility of such an enormous loss is very difficult, but face it infertile couples must.

Some people think that getting a baby —by birth or by adoption —is the resolution to infertility. Such simple answers tend to overlook and even negate the impact of the losses of infertility by suggesting that physical substitution will solve its problems. Infertility's losses are more complicated than that. So strongly does this crisis affect our lives, often for such an extended period of time, that feelings about infertility cannot be expected to go away with the announcement of a pregnancy or the arrival of a child.

Resolution is the emotional process of first coming to grips with the reality that long-held assumptions may be incorrect, and then dealing with the stress, fear, and even panic that this realization may cause. After confronting this reality head on, resolution requires looking at alternatives as carefully and objectively as possible in order to make positive and productive decisions. The process of resolution takes time; and time, often seen as the enemy during the medical treatment process, can be an ally in the emotional process of resolution. Time allows us to muster coping resources, to sift through confusion, and to build bridges to communication.

Couples may react quite differently to the reality of infertility because each individual and each relationship is unique. The depth of loss each person feels may vary from major frustration in some to obsessive depression in others, with most people falling somewhere in the middle of this spectrum. Degrees of reaction will be colored by a variety of factors, including the length of time spent dealing medically with infertility, the quality of understanding received from professionals, the strength of the network of family and friends, and coping patterns built over a lifetime.

Infertility doesn't represent a single potential loss, but rather a number of losses. Though infertile people must each face the potential of all of these losses, each of them tends to react most deeply to one particular loss. That one loss the individual must mourn. Some of infertility's potential losses are:

1. The loss of individual genetic continuity and an unbroken family blood line.

2. The loss of a jointly conceived child.

3. The loss of the physical satisfaction of the pregnancy/ birth experience.

4. The loss of the emotional gratifications of a shared birth/breastfeeding experience and the mystical goal of parent/child bonding at birth.

5. The loss of the opportunity to parent.

6. The loss of control.

Further complicating the infertile couple's ability to recognize and thus to deal effectively with their personal losses are the attendant losses which often accompany infertility —the losses of self-esteem and self-worth. When we don't like and value ourselves as we are, we usually stop feeling confident and competent. These extra losses, then, make it difficult for infertile couples to trust their own judgment in evaluating their alternatives both medical and non-medical. Since the most deeply felt losses of husbands and wives are often different, it can be troublesome for spouses to support one another. As well, faced with different losses, the couple finds it perplexing to objectively sort through their options, as many of the options that alleviate one loss aggravate another!

In working toward resolution it is important that infertile couples try to determine which of infertility's losses each is feeling most deeply and to recognize that since the losses each of them mourn are likely to be different, the decision making they face in determining which of their alternatives is most appropriate will demand sensitive, intensive and careful communication and readiness to compromise. For example, the person who fears and mourns most deeply the loss of the possibility of parenting can indeed avoid the finality of this loss by using one of the child producing alternatives: adoption, donor insemination, surrogate mothering. The man who mourns most deeply the loss of his genetic continuity or the woman who mourns the loss of the pregnancy experience cannot resolve these losses by adopting. The person who has been raised to assume that if he or she works hard enough anything is possible may mourn the loss of control. For such a person turning control over to an adoption caseworker may be quite painful, while determinedly seeking out a child through private adoption may allow the reestablishment of that lost sense of control.

Every couple's fertility problem is unique —owned only by them and experienced differently from any other couple experiencing infertility. For some the study itself, with its completely unspontaneous routine of basal body temperature charts, invasive and uncomfortable tests, and scheduled intercourse may be so stressful that a diagnosis of absolute sterility may come as a kind of relief. For others, the study may allow a harbored sense of optimism that prevents their being intruded upon and stressed, so that they are unprepared for a final diagnosis that is unfavorable and collapse under its weight.

Still, because the infertility experience usually means working through a loss reaction, there are similarities between the experiences of most infertile couples. Typically a first reaction to suspected infertility is surprise. As has been mentioned, adults of this first birth control generation expect fertility to be controllable, and they have often spent a number of their potentially most fertile years trying diligently not to get pregnant.

For a while, many couples are likely to deny to themselves that there really is a problem. After all, John's job takes him out of town a lot, and they both work really long hours . . . maybe they just haven't been hitting the right days. Mom's advice to relax because they've been trying too hard, the friend's suggestion that they have a glass of wine before bedtime, seem logical to a couple using denial to muster their coping resources. Sometimes it's only after coming back from that vacation that was supposed to result in a pregnancy that denial is put behind them and the couple seeks help. Sometimes, though, further denial is then encouraged by a doctor, who, without beginning a workup in earnest or referring them beyond himself for one, suggests that they are still young and healthy and they should give it some more time.

It's when others deny their problem even after they themselves have ceased to do so that the infertile couple begins to isolate themselves. Confronted by bulging bellies and the blooming trees of a fertile world, the activities which seem impossibly centered on the children which elude them, and feeling intensely guilty about a variety of forbidden thoughts —hatred of pregnant strangers, jealousy of a sister's new baby, secret pleasure when Fertile Myrtle miscarries —such a couple needs permission to avoid the painful reminders of their infertility for a time, staying away from baby showers, christenings, some family gatherings. When family and friends can't understand such needs and instead label such behavior as irrationally moody, the infertile couple needs other infertile people to support their normalcy.

Together and yet alone, the infertile couple deals with intensive issues. No matter which partner has the medical diagnosis of a fertility problem, both partners, since they love one another and see each other as permanent partners, face the possibility of not reproducing. Their sexuality, then, already battered by the schedules and invasions of testing and treatment, may be called into question. With spontaneity gone, for most couples a time may come when all interest in sex is lost for a while. An unplanned and undiscussed moratorium may be called, for communication is often less than optimum when partners deal not only with the couple's issues but with the individual pain that infertility brings. Thus the sudden unexplained loss of sexual interest by one partner may frighten the other, who is left wondering if s/he has become unattractive to the spouse or if the condition might be permanent . . . wondering if, in fact, being infertile might mean being asexual. A couple at such a point needs assurance of the normalcy and predictability of their situation, but this is difficult for them to find if they do not know about infertility-oriented groups or have been led to believe by misinformed professionals that such groups are for the "last-ditch, no-hope" couples.

It isn't at all unusual for an infertile couple to become obsessed with their infertility for a time. After all, every aspect of their lives, from the small decisions about whether to buy jockey shorts or boxers or whether to accept a dinner invitation for next month on what might turn out to be THE night to the large ones like whether to accept a job transfer that might mean changing doctors or losing a place on an adoption list or whether to buy a house in the suburbs with sidewalks for trikes as opposed to a condo in the city close to jobs, is colored by their failure to conceive. And because from a treatment perspective the 1980's is the best time ever to be infertile, it has become increasingly difficult for couples to know when to stop. Their own obsession is fed, then, by the unlikely successes of others who seem to have gone the extra mile.

What is most difficult about an obsession is that it can block a healthy resolution by short-circuiting logic. It is when a couple is obsessed with infertility that they begin to believe that getting a baby —any baby and from any source, as quickly as possible and at whatever physical, emotional, or financial costs —will resolve their infertility. Such couples are likely to ask to go beyond what their doctors see as safe limits in using drugs, will volunteer for third or fourth surgeries though chances of success seem abysmally low, they will consider surrogate mothering or black market adoptions, and, because of their short-circuited logic, they may insist upon seeing donor sperm as medicine to cure a husband's low sperm count rather than as an alternative producing a kind of adoption.

Getting stuck obsessively in any stage of infertility is very easy, because infertility makes one angry —angry at oneself or at a spouse or at God or at a professional. Sometimes the anger is logically directed in response to insensitivity or a mistake, but often couples can feel so cheated in their struggle with infertility that they rail irrationally at innocent bystanders.

The anger eventually turns to bargaining, dredging up the past and working through guilty thoughts as the couple seeks some reasonable explanation for being punished with infertility. They may return to the magical thinking of childhood ("If only I had . . .". "If only we hadn't . . ."). Sometimes the infertile couple will find that their religious beliefs are called into question. Those raised in the Judeo-Christian tradition and familiar with the stories of the Bible's barren women —Sarah, Rachel, Hannah, Leah, Elizabeth —may misinterpret these stories or have them misinterpretted by others and come to feel that only by finding favor with God will they conceive. Two books which may be of help to couples dealing with their spirituality as it relates to their infertility are *When Bad Things Happen To Good People* by Rabbi Harold Kushner (Schocken Books, 1981) and *Coping With Infertility* by Judith Stigger (Augsberg Publishers, 1983).

Nearly all couples faced with a fertility impairment will come through the stages of **surprise, denial, anger, bargaining, isolation** in some sequence of their own, and many of them will have experienced an **obsession.** There remains, however, one stage in the loss reaction chain that only those couples who have come to see themselves as permanently infertile (whether through medical diagnosis or personal decision that enough is enough) will face. In the loss spectrum this has been called **depression.** The infertility experience, however, is full of depression. It is so time consuming a condition and contains so many ups and downs on the cyclical roller coaster of hope and crashing despair of monthly treatments, that depression for some seems to become a way of life. Because this particular depression is more sustained and pervasive than the earlier ones, I have preferred to rename this stage **The Burial.**

As this stage settles in, bringing with it despair, lethargy, distress, there may be irrational behavior changes, a loss of appetite, inability to sleep or the need to sleep all the time. Though a couple may have been moving through the loss cycle for some time, the final realization that there is to be no jointly conceived child is still likely to come as a shock. There may be a great deal of emotional drifting. All of the previously experienced emotions —anger, guilt, lack of control —may crash back in and be re-experienced. The couple will mourn the loss of the child of their assumptions, the one whose face they had each begun to conjure back in the days of childhood play. This child will have to be buried, along with an assortment of related fantasies. The manner in which the couple would reveal the pregnancy to others, how they would have enjoyed shopping for maternity clothes and nursery items, the excitement of going through prepared childbirth classes and a perfect delivery experience —all will need to be buried. The child with his father's nose, mother's eyes, and an assortment of traits both desirable and undesirable from both families will not be born. The couple will wonder if life can go on, if anything can ever be the same again.

Time and understanding support will help a couple through this stage, too. And, having passed through the crisis, they will come to see that life can go on, and happily, but that it will never be quite the same again. Having buried their assumptions, such a couple will be ready to look for a way around the blockage in their life's goal and will find energy to clearly examine their options.

Some couples who are infertile will decide that adoption is an appropriate alternative for them. Someplace along the way they will have put their names on an adoption list. The waiting is hard, but eventually an agency will notify them that it is time for a homestudy to begin. More than likely today they will be assigned to a caseworker who knows at least something about the theoretical loss reaction to infertility. Too often this caseworker's knowledge is incomplete, however, and her assumptions may be that in order to adopt, the couple must have put their infertility entirely behind them, that in order to be considered ready to adopt, the pain of infertility must be a thing of the past.

The emotional goal of resolution is worked through slowly over a very long period of time for many couples. The process of grieving, the cyclical depression of infertility, most often begins not after a couple has been given a final diagnosis, but during the testing and treatment process. Unless infertility comes as a result of a sudden and unexpected medical condition (hysterectomy or testicular cancer, for instance) the realization of loss is slow in coming and slow to be resolved. Such a loss is a handicap, but is often an unsupported and invisible one. Thus, for couples for whom infertility is to be permanent, the loss is integrated in stages, each one building upon the one before. Infertility is a profound emotional experience and it doesn't just go away. As with any wound, it heals with a scar which can be opened again at an unexpected time. Infertility's scars remain on the soul long after the wounds have healed. For many couples adoption is part of the resolution process. The key becomes, then, to properly prepare them for this stage and to ensure that they have not left unfinished business behind them in the resolution process.

1. Smith Jerome, and Franklin I. Miroff, *You're Our Child: A Social/Psychological Approach to Adoption;* Lanham, MD: University Press of America, 1981, p. 18.

2. Feigelman, William and Arnold R. Silverman, *Chosen Children.* New York: Praeger, 1983, p. 62.

3. Colgrove, Melba, Harold H. Bloomfield, and Peter McWilliams, *How to Survive the Loss of a Love.* New York: Bantam Books, 1976, p. 16.

4. Sheehy, Gail; *Passages.* New York: E.P. Dutton, 1974, p. 21.

CHAPTER 4

ADOPTIVE PARENTING IS DIFFERENT

Lullaby for an Adopted Child
by E. Van Clef

Hush my baby - do not cry
Mama will sing you a lullaby.
Hush my baby, I know your pain.
I hear - your cries are not in vain.

Shh- I know-

Adoption is non-consensual.
No one asked you- Child- do you take these parents.
No one asked you- Child- Do you wish to be
to exist
to be born.
No, all this happened without your consent.
Poor Child- I know your pain-
Infertility is also nonconsensual.

Shh- I know-

Adoption is violent.
It rips apart ties that bind parent and child.
It strips you of your lineage and heritage.
It leaves you standing alone.
Poor Child- I know your pain-
Infertility is also violent.

Hush my child- hold tight to me.
Let's not think on what cannot be.
Let's think instead of love's power to heal-
And to each other bond and cling come what will.

The second task in developing a sense of entitlement in adoption-built families is the task of coming to recognize that adoptive parenting is different from biological parenting in a number of significant and unavoidable ways. H. David Kirk, in *Shared Fate* and *Adoptive Kinship,* discusses this task at length. Kirk theorizes that all of us come to adulthood with a certain set of roles we expect to fill in life, each of which carries with it a set of societal expectations. When we assume a life role without assuming with it all of the role's expectations, we experience a **role handicap**. The roles of parent and child in adoption-built families, says Kirk, are both handicapped, and families tend to cope with handicaps psychologically in one of two ways —either by acknowledging the differences that the handicap brings or by rejecting the differences entirely.

Kirk, and Smith and Miroff, believe that healthy parenting in adoption can only occur in families which acknowledge the differences in adoption, and in doing so accept that both parents and children, while deriving substantial gains from this life experience, also experience significant losses in adoption. Such an acknowledgement helps these families to develop mutual compassion and understanding that will strengthen the family bond by enhancing the family members' ability to communicate. This concept, which Kirk has called the **Shared Fate theory**, contends that the warmest, closest, and healthiest family relationships are built when family members feel a sense of authenticity about their relationship (a sense of entitlement), are able to empathize with one another, and communicate openly and well.

Because society has the expectation that families are only biologically built (one of the unmet expectations that causes adoption-built families to experience a role handicap), adoption-built families have in the past been encouraged to pretend that their families are "just the same" as biological families. The problem this caused was that while adoptive families and intermediaries were busy trying to convince themselves that there were no significant differences in adoption, society wasn't accepting that idea at all. In North

America, then, we have moved through a series of professionally endorsed attitudes toward how adoptive families should deal with themselves.

First it was "Take him and love him as your own. There are no differences. But don't tell anybody about the adoption — including the child." Pre-adoptive mothers therefore pretended to be pregnant, sometimes went off on "trips" for a number of weeks, and returned with a new baby who often looked older than he was supposed to be. The family told no one about the adoption and allowed the child along with everyone else to believe that they had given birth to him. Keeping such a deep dark family secret, however, is next to impossible, so often somebody was told, who told somebody else, who told somebody else, who let it slip to the adoptee, who by that time usually was an older child or an adult. Typically the adoptee's reaction to this news was surprise, anger, humiliation, and distrust. ("If they didn't tell me this, what else don't I know?") The parents' reaction to being confronted with their child's new knowledge was often horror and embarrassment and a refusal to share any details with the adoptee.

When this approach proved faulty, professional advice became, "Take him and love him as your own. There's no difference. But be sure to tell him about the adoption." And so families were encouraged to reveal the adoption, but weren't really helped to see why or how to do so. They accepted in principle the need to tell, but followed the prescription rather mechanically —as a kind of ritual that had no depth or meaning for them. Adoptive parents avoided dealing with the realities of adoption because it hurt for them to do so. In the short term it was easier to forget the differences in adoption, and since the professional community had not pointed out to them any long term benefits for acknowledging the differences, they simply "did their duty" by having the required "talk" with their children and then returned to the much more comfortable role of pretending that their families were no different than biological familie⁻

However, adoption **is** different —different in a number of very important ways. No matter how hard we try to believe that adoption is the same as giving birth to a child, Kirk points out that we have only to look at the laws on which adoption is based to see that it is not the same:

1. Only adoptees are denied access to their birth records.

2. Inheritance in adoption-built families comes only through parents, not through extended adoptive families, unless the adoptees are specifically named in the will.

3. Similarly, life insurance benefits are not passed on to adoptees unless they are specifically named as beneficiaries.

4. Incest and intermarriage laws in some states do not apply to adoptees. [1]

The lack of a biological tie to a family not educated and supported to feel good about their differences can lead each family member to see their ties as being constantly in jeopardy. Only when adoption-built families come to see their relationship as being different from but not inferior to biological relationships can they build positive relationships which are based on their uniqueness.

The Shared Fate theory suggests that in a consistently loving relationship which acknowledges the differences families will have an orientation toward openness, risk taking, trust, and clarity of expectations that is based on their constantly acknowledged empathy for one another's societally perceived loss. Such empathy will produce in the parents a readiness to listen to the child's questions about his background even though such questions may at times be troublesome to the parents. This parental readiness to listen and to understand will enhance the child's sense of trust in the parents. Therefore, the bonds between parents and child will be strengthened.

In practical fact, nearly every adoptive family veers back and forth between acknowledgment of differences and rejection of differences as coping patterns. What tends to happen is that the family acknowledges the differences in situations which are comfortable and easy, and, as issues come closer and closer to the painful core, where parents need to acknowledge their personal losses, they become more likely to begin to reject differences.

Because even today adoptive parents are told to tell but are not helped to see clearly how the short term discomforts of constant and careful acknowledgment of differences will benefit their families in the long run, families who for the most part reject the differences are common. Most of these families who reject the differences in adoption have adopted infants. They don't belong to parents' groups because they "aren't having any problems and don't need a group" In the instances where such families do belong to adoption-oriented groups, often the groups themselves encourage rejection of differences in adoptive parenting and are focused on fear of open records or open adoption —a need to protect themselves as families —rather than on positive experiences for their children. Such parents don't read much about adoption. They rarely attend adoption-oriented work-shops even though they might very well have done so as preadoptive couples.

On the other hand, those who adopt foreign born or American special needs children are as a group much more likely to acknowledge the differences consistently. For one reason, they have little choice. There is no way they can pretend that their families aren't different because society can see quite clearly their differences. As well, agencies are much more likely to have prepared them well for these differences and to have encouraged them to acknowledge differences from the outset since the prejudices they will face are more widespread and openly acknowledged.

These parents form groups: OURS, Families Adopting Children Everywhere, Project Orphans Abroad, Latin

American Parents Association. Most of the member groups of the North American Council on Adoptable Children are made up primarily of non-traditional families. Recently such groups have found that families who had adopted healthy infants and rejected the differences in adoption, ignoring the parent group during their early years as parents, have begun to seek out such groups as their children have reached pre-adolescence. These kids are quite different from the kids of the families who have been with the group since the children joined the family. The kids from the families who have consistently acknowledged differences are at ease and open about their adoptive status. The families who have rejected the differences are more likely to be somewhat anxious and closed.

Infertile adoptive parents are not superhuman. They must be expected to regress sometimes when dealing with their unique families. While all families will use rejection-of-differences behavior sometimes, it is most important that they be encouraged to acknowledge differences most of the time. They will do so if they can be helped to see the benefits of this approach to parenting in adoption.

What adopting families need is point-by-point education. In order to get this, however, some re-education in this area is most important. It needs to begin with social workers, whose own values and training have in some cases tended to encourage rejection-of-differences behavior. This in itself may be difficult, because what must be faced is that acceptance of differences may ultimately bring much more openness to adoption in general, placing more control in the hands of birth and adoptive parents rather than agencies.

The miracle of watching a child grow brings both pleasure and pain to his parents. Becoming a parent is indeed a humbling experience. For the willing and eager parent by birth, however, the humbleness is tinged as well with pride in a personal accomplishment. He has only himself, his partner, and God to thank for the gift of his child. The traditional adoptor, too, is humbled by the prospect of parenthood. His humbleness, though, is tinged not with pride, but with sadness and perhaps with humiliation, as he confronts once again his own infertility, and his indebtedness not just to God, but to an agency, a social worker, and a set of birthparents for the gift of his child. Since many infertile couples unrealistically expected to put infertility permanently behind them with adoption, they may find that entitlement-building is a slower experience than they expected hinged on their coming to feel the authenticity of their parenthood. It is sometimes difficult for them to allay their greatest fear, that in the trend toward more openness and communication between birth and adoptive parents, adoption will somehow be reduced to 18 years of babysitting rather than "real" parenting.

In reality any form of parenting is a kind of custodial care. The poet Kahlil Gibran pointed this out early in the century in his poem *On Children*:

> And a woman who held a babe against her bosom said, speak to us of children.
> And he said:
>
> Your children are not your children.
> They are the sons and daughters of Life's longing for itself.
> They come through you but not from you.
> And though they are with you, yet they belong not to you.
>
> You may give them your love but not your thoughts.
> For they have their own thoughts.
> You may house their bodies, but not their souls,
> For their souls dwell in the house of tomorrow, which you cannot visit, not even in your dreams.
> You may strive to be like them, but seek not to make them like you.
> For life goes not backward nor tarries with yesterday.

> You are the bows from which your children as living
> arrows are sent forth.
> The archer sees the mark upon the path of the infinite, and
> He bends you with His might that His arrows might go
> swift and far.
> Let your bending in the archer's hand be for gladness,
> For even as He loves the arrow that flies, so He loves also
> the bow that is stable.

We don't own our children, and we have no guarantee of
our children's eventual loyalty to their families as adults. Just
as it is a gamble taken by all of us who choose to rear children,
whether they come to us by birth or by adoption, it is one of
the risks of the relationship that acknowledges adoption's
differences.

Kirk suggests that there are a number of factors about
adoption-built families that might make them more appropriate role models for the family of the future:

1. Families are becoming smaller (one or two children), as
   adoptive families have been traditionally sized.

2. Infertility results in a gender equality in parenting roles,
   so that there is often a lack of division of labor by
   gender.

3. Adoptive parents have traditionally been older than the
   average parent by birth, a circumstance parallel to the
   current societal tendency to delay childbearing.

4. Adoptive families have always had to contend with the
   overlapping loyalties and demands of an adoptee's
   having two sets of parents. This is similar to the
   increasing situation of step families formed as divorce
   and remarriage increases.

According to Kirk, then, what may come to be the major
support system for the family of the future may be what

basically has always supported families built by adoption —
authenticity, empathy, and communication. [2]

As well, in helping families to understand the many
benefits of consistently acknowledging adoption's differences we will help them —in what I see as an extension of
The Shared Fate Theory —to become more empathetic to
and less threatened by birthparents, a change that can only
enhance the feelings of self-worth of the adoptee and
strengthen the family's bonds of love.

Adoptors, then, must be educated to understand that
people are most inclined to stay in relationships in which
they know that they are free to leave. This is a constant theme
in literature throughout centuries, from the old proverb
"There are two great gifts we can give our children. One is
roots, the other wings," to the modern day Glen Campbell
song "Gentle On My Mind," which tells of a man whose
decision to stay is based on "knowin' I'm not shackled by
forgotten words and bonds and the ink stains that have dried
upon some line. . ."

1. Kirk, H. David, *Adoptive Kinship*. Toronto: Butterworths,
Chapter 8.

2. Ibid, Chapter 8.

CHAPTER 5

SOCIETY'S FEELINGS ABOUT ADOPTION

Not Really Yours
by Vicki Andres

Not really yours, some people say,
And you'll find out some bitter day.
She'll turn from you and then you'll know
The words I speak now to be true.
Spare yourself the tears, my friend,
of giving of your heart.
Spare yourself the grief and pain
of being ripped apart.

Not really mine? You utter fool!
Yes, we'll know bitter days and cruel
And turning away from and turning back,
Of tears and pain there'll be no lack.

But where is love except such things?
There is no joy like giving brings.
To take your child and share your soul
Rips not apart, but makes a whole.

The third task in building a sense of entitlement —learning to handle the questions and comments of outsiders which will reflect society's less than positive feeling about adoption —is quite heavily influenced by how far the family has come in accomplishing the first two tasks. This is another task for which families would sometimes prefer to deny a need.

Society in general, and even a number of the professionals who work in the field of adoption, see adoption as a second best alternative for all involved. It is second best for adoptive parents, because the children are not "their own;" second best for children who have been adopted, who will be separated from "their real families;" and second best for birthparents, who prove themselves less than adequate as human beings by "giving away their own flesh and blood."

Many people think some or all of the following thoughts at some time:

1. Birthparents are irresponsible sleep arounds —tramps.

2. No worthy civilized person would be able to give up his own flesh and blood.

3. Birthparents can, will, and should forget.

4. The only acceptable reason not to parent a child you give birth to is that you are too young . . . and in such cases other family members should assume the responsibility.

5. REAL parents give birth.

6. REAL children are not adopted.

7. Adoption is family building the easy way.

8. Adoption is a second best alternative, because the kids don't have REAL families and the adoptive parents have no kids of their own.

9. The only acceptable reason to adopt is infertility.

10. You can't REALLY love a child you don't give birth to.

11. REAL attachment can take place only at birth.

12. Adoptees are less healthy emotionally than are other people.

13. Adoptees wouldn't search if they REALLY loved their adoptive families.

14. Adoptees are lucky that someone as good as their adoptive parents was willing to take them in when their REAL parents rejected them.

A generation ago the adoption scene was quite different than it is today. At that point in time the only societally acceptable way of dealing with an untimely pregnancy was to make an adoption plan after going away to deliver the child in secret. At that point in time the issue of childlessness, if not the issue of infertility, was relatively easily and quickly remedied by adoption. The number of healthy infants far exceeded the demand of adoptors. Adoptors, then, regained control of their lives by actually selecting their own child, choosing from a menu of physical, intellectual, sociological and ethnic qualities a child perfectly "matched" to their families. The role of the agency in those days seemed to be to find the right blue ribbon baby for the right blue ribbon family.

This situation could not be further from today's reality. Today fewer than five in one hundred young women dealing with an unplanned pregnancy make adoption plans for their babies. Some of the other ninety-five elect to have legal abortions, but the majority of them choose to parent their children themselves, quite often with public assistance. This state of affairs cannot be seen as all good or all bad from any perspective. Certainly we can be glad to have grown more tolerant as a society and to see that single parenthood can be and often is very healthy. We can be pleased that we have come to see that individuals need to make their own choices rather than to have them made for them by institutions. As a principle, most people would probably agree that adoption is not always a good alternative and would support informed choice for people needing to make decisions about their options in dealing with an untimely pregnancy.

In practice, however, counseling seems to have swung

from the extreme of mandating adoption twenty years ago to counseling against it today. Societal pressures have caused a shift of thinking that in many instances has made it next to impossible for birthparents to make adoption plans for their children today. Considering the discouraging statistics which indicate that teen mothers lead difficult lives, undereducated and under-employed for a lifetime as compared to their non-parent contemporaries; that children of such parents are less likely to complete schooling, more likely to be abused and neglected, etc.; this shift can't be seen as all good, either.

All of this has resulted in a dramatic difference today in the number and kind of children available for adoption. Forty couples wait an average of three to six years to adopt each infant for whom an adoption plan is made. On the other hand, well over 100,000 children wait in America today for permanent homes. These older, handicapped children, often in sibling groups, are children who might never even have been a part of "the system" a generation ago. Young parents who try to parent babies often find that their children become part of the adoption system much later after they themselves have come to see that they are unable to parent them in ways which they see as adequate or after their parental rights have been terminated due to neglect or abuse. On the other hand, this "worship of the womb," as Dorothy Debolt called it in her keynote address to the 1984 NACAC Conference, is also in part responsible for judges' reluctance to terminate parental rights in situations of abuse and neglect and to instead repeatedly return children to dangerous environments. We've become a society where it is not acceptable to make an adoption plan for a healthy infant, but it is somehow more acceptable to abort them or to "throw away" older children or children with handicaps of some sort. How did we get to such a place?

We live in a time when the stability of the family as an institution is questionable. For much of this century changes in social attitudes and structure have nibbled away at the foundations of the family as it had come to be accepted in the western world. In reaction to these frightening changes, a number of researchers and educators have sought ways to reinforce the concept of familiness. Many of the suggestions they've made have become part of a movement called family-centeredness. Though without formal structure, this loose coalition of researchers, educators and groups has included the prepared childbirth movement (Dick-Read, Bradley, Lamaze, LeBoyer), the mothering advocates (LaLeche League, etc.) and bonding/attachment theorists (Klaus and Kennell, et al.) The movement has had a profound and largely positive impact on familiness. One of the most important results of the acceptance of this collective philosophy has been a generation of fathers who are likely to be as physically and emotionally involved with their children as mothers traditionally have been.

Unfortunately, however, the original goals of each of these educators/researchers (to make families better) has been widely misinterpreted so that large segments of society now believe that without each of a number of prescribed elements in place (a positive pregnancy experience, father-involved "natural" childbirth, delivery area "bonding," breastfeeding, and so on) a family is somehow less _real_, not quite as _good_ as it might have been. A romantic mysticism has developed around the physical process of motherhood and the mother/child relationship that has confused and upset many people. Those who need a caesarean delivery after prepared childbirth training, those whose pregnancies and deliveries are difficult and demand medical intervention, those who are separated from a child at birth because of illness, prematurity, or foster care, those who are unable to or choose not to breastfeed, those who are unable or choose not to become pregnant and consider adoption, those who give birth to a child they decide not to parent but to make an adoption plan for, are allowed and encouraged to feel guilty, disappointed, and painfully second rate.

A number of researchers have begun to question the effects of delivery room interaction on long term parent/child relationships. There have been no findings that indicate that the positive effects of early maternal/child contact carry over to enhance a more positive relationship between mothers and children beyond the newborn stage. Some of the researchers themselves have tried (to little avail) to caution professionals and lay groups that their writings can be and have been misinterpreted. Cautionary voices have gone largely ignored. It will take years and a great deal of consistent vocalness from a variety of persons to correct the damage done by his misinterpretation without taking away the positive impact of the family-centeredness movement.

In the meantime, for both birthparents and potential parents exploring adoption as part of their family planning, this influence affects their self-esteem and self-worth by reinforcing the "unacceptability" of their situations. Subsequently their decision making abilities are undermined by their lack of confidence in themselves.

The family-centeredness movement is so widespread that relatively few persons are uninfluenced by it. Even adoption professionals may know just enough about the various theories intertwined in this movement to make misjudgments and misinterpretations that eventually have damaging effects upon their primary clients —children. Is foster parenting different enough from biological or adoptive parenting that foster parents of infants need training? Can an infant of just a few weeks "bond" to a foster parent to such an extent that disengagement and reattachment therapy will be necessary for the child and his permanent family? The answers to each of these questions is "yes," but widespread practice in agencies around the country does not reflect their acceptance of these facts.

Those not personally involved in it often do not understand the social process that is adoption. Even the most widely divergent of adoption interested groups of birthparents, adoptive parents, and adoptees can agree with this statement. To most, adoption is an anomaly. Because each of us at times wishes that we could discard who we are and begin again, we are fearful of something that appears to have been formed in just such a manner. Adoption-built families just don't seem **real**.

And what is **real**? Do you remember the classic nursery story *The Velveteen Rabbit* by Margery Williams? In it a stuffed rabbit longs to achieve the special status afforded only the best loved toys — realness.

> "What is REAL?" asked the Rabbit one day, when they were lying side by side near the nursery fender, before Nana came to tidy the room. "Does it mean having things that buzz inside you and a stick-out handle?"
>
> "Real isn't how you are made," said the Skin Horse. "It's a thing that happens to you. When a child loves you for a long, long time, not just to play with, but REALLY loves you, then you become Real."
>
> "Does it hurt?" asked the Rabbit.
>
> "Sometimes," said the Skin Horse, for he was always truthful. "When you are REAL you don't mind being hurt." [1]

Much of what can be done to help adoptive families accomplish the third task in building a sense of entitlement —learning to deal with the questions and comments that reflect a negative view of adoption —would also help birthparents feel more comfortable exploring the adoption alternative. It involves our becoming adoption advocates, learning to correct adoption mythology rampant in society at large and to use ourselves and to help others to use positive adoption language rather than negative adoption language. It involves our helping society at large to accept the **realness**, the authenticity, of adoption-built families.

Blood alone does not make a family. Families in our culture are built in several ways: by blood, by law, by love, and by social custom. Take for example the husband and wife —unrelated by blood they are considered a family by reason of love and law. A woman and her sister-in-law, unrelated by blood, are considered part of the same family by social custom. Society does not consider the familiness of either of these two pairs unusual or less than **real**. So we must begin to help them accept adoption-built families. There are a number of ways in which we can do this:

1. We can become more assertive in correcting misinterpretations about families, whether built by birth or adoption.

2. We must use positive, non-loaded adoption language consistently and encourage others to do so. (For example "their children" rather than "their adopted child" and "one of their own;" "birthparents" as opposed to "real parents;" "made an adoption plan" rather than "gave up," "put up," "surrendered," or "relinquished;" "meeting" rather than "reunion.") The best discussion I have seen of positive adoption language is in Marietta Spencer's booklet *Understanding Adoption As A Family Building Option* from the multi-media curriculum "Adoption Builds Families." (See resources.)

3. We must not ourselves nor should we allow others to stereotype any members of the adoption triad. We must recognize and help others to recognize that some birthparents abandoned their children and some had them torn away from them without choice, that some of them long throughout their lives to meet, to know and to hold their children, and others haven't really thought much about those children again; that some adolescent adoptees struggle more than the average adolescent with their identities and some do not, that some need to search and some don't; that some adoptive parents are great at parenting and others fail, that some can accept different special needs than others can accept and some can accept none at all, that as parents they can be just as REAL and just as WRONG as any other parents.

4. We must offer adoption-built and adoption-separated families appropriate support and education both pre and post placement and we must educate society at large on a continuing basis.

If we want others to see adoptive families as **real**, we ourselves must believe that they are. When adoptive parents have built a sense of entitlement to their children (resolving infertility or motivational issues, accepting that adoption is significantly different from biological parenting, and dealing with societal reservations about this method of family building) their children, too, will feel this authenticity about their families.

"Wasn't I Real before?" asked the little Rabbit.

"You were Real to the Boy," the Fairy said, "because he loved you. Now you shall be Real to everyone." [2]

---

1. Williams, Margery, *The Velveteen Rabbit.*

2. Williams, Margery, *The Velveteen Rabbit.*

CHAPTER 6

WORKING IT THROUGH

By involving themselves in a well designed homestudy and in making a commitment to immersing themselves in adoption, using groups, seminars and reading materials, it is possible that adoptive parents might approach completion of the three tasks assigned by Smith and Miroff to entitlement-building even before placement. Strong progress in each area is considered imperative.

All parents, whether they give birth to or adopt their children, must accomplish another task: the physical and emotional process of actually **claiming** a particular child as their own. For parents who give birth to a child they will raise, this step begins during the pregnancy. For adoptive parents it cannot begin until a particular child has been identified as the one they will parent.

Bonding theorists have noted a number of behaviors common to humans as they meet their newborn child, including stroking his body; nuzzling, sniffing and kissing him; examining and counting fingers and toes, etc. Social workers have noted similar behaviors with adoptive parents. Often couples prefer to bring along clothing for the child to wear home when they meet their baby. This, too, is an initial claiming behavior.

The claiming process may be complicated for adoptive parents by a number of factors, including the appearance of the child, the age of the child, their feelings about the child's genetic background, their feelings about their child's social history, their reactions to the child's personality, and so on.

One of the ways that all parents claim their children is in establishing their own parenting style. When adoptive parents bring a newborn home from the hospital this is a relatively easy step for them to accomplish in the claiming process, in that the child has known no other parenting style that might interfere with his adjusting to the style of his new parents.

However, many infants are not placed straight from the hospital. Often they spend precious days, weeks, or months in foster care. Why? Sometimes birthparents are not ready to terminate parental rights. Sometimes the birthfather has not been identified and the agency prefers to terminate the unknown father's rights before placement. Sometimes the birthparents do not agree with one another on the adoption plan. Sometimes the agency has not been counseling the birthparents for a long enough time before the child's birth for them to feel that the parents are adequately prepared to give consent to adoption. Sometimes factors in the birthparents' medical history suggest the possibility of a problem that the agency would prefer to rule out or identify before making a placement. Sometimes the child's race or health or requirements of the birthparents make a child more difficult to place. Sometimes "administrivia" keeps agency workers from arranging court dates for termination hearings as quickly as they are typically arranged in private adoptions.

Adoption workers who advocate for the continued use of routine foster care in such cases cite at least three benefits of foster care: it gives birthparents more time in which to make their decision, it protects adoptive parents from the possibility of various kinds of disappointments, it gives workers more time to make good placement choices. No studies have supported these statements as beneficial in the long run to the primary client: the child. The decision to make an adoption plan does not become more or less easy given time. It will always be a difficult decision and even after the decision for or against adoption has been made most birthparents will experience periods in their lives when they will question their own decision. Adoptive parents may often be more protected than they wish to be. Many of them would prefer to "risk" an unlikely medical condition just as they would in giving birth to a child rather than to lose precious time with him. Many of these so-called risks are nebulous at any rate, and many pediatricians feel that the likelihood of a serious potential problem not identifiable soon after birth becoming identifiable in four to six weeks is small. In accepting the realities of adoption, potential adoptors must also accept the realities of parenthood —there are no guarantees that a child apparently healthy at birth will not develop problems later. Adoption workers usually have social and medical histories for birthmothers and potential adoptive parents before a child is born. Thus "matches" can and should be made before a birth. Waiting until after a child is born to make such decisions or to initiate searches in the case of previously known unusual circumstances is a form of procrastination that ill serves birthparents, adoptive parents and adoptees, but is still common practice at many agencies.

Many important decisions are made in the early days of life that establish parenting style and infant habits. What formula? What pacifier or none at all? Breast or bottle feeding? These are decisions which are usually the right of a parent to make. Not allowing parents to make these decisions themselves but forcing them instead to adapt to a style of parenting already established by a foster caretaker wrenches control from the adoptors and limits the ways in which they can claim their child. Forcing them to compromise their parenting preferences in this way further reinforces the feeling that the child isn't "really" theirs, which may cause resentments to develop, delaying the attachment/entitlement process.

"He eats every four hours and I've been nursing him in between when he gets fussy. He's never had a pacifier. We rock him to sleep. I use this brand of infant carrier and I usually wear him around in it all morning. These nipples are the ones that he's used to. I bathe him in the evening. He's used to taking his last bottle around 11:30 because that's when my husband gets home. We take him for a walk after dinner and that puts him to sleep. He's been sleeping with us. He's been held a lot because our kids love to carry him around." These statements reflect habits developed in a baby —habits initiated not by the infant, but by his caretakers. They reflect small, lifestyle-influenced decisions normally made by parents.

Though social workers acknowledge that bonding and

attachment do occur and that a final placement should optimally be made early enough to avoid attachment disruptions, too often they use as a guide some arbitrary age, allowing themselves one month, two months, three months, before they believe that bonding can become a "problem." In reality bonding is a highly individual process. Some babies will make apparently easy transitions at several months of age, while others will have difficulty adapting to change after just a week or two. Experience with older children who have experienced multiple placements has provided a wealth of material on the necessity for appropriate disengagement preparation and reattachment therapy. Vera Fahlberg, Claudia Jewett, Kay Donley and other professionals have demonstrated that when these steps are not properly executed with older children, severe problems may result. Tiny infants, too, can experience the "kidnap syndrome" of being moved from one secure placement to another without proper preparation. Why, then, subject newborns to this possibility if there are ways to avoid foster care?

The existence of a foster caretaker may also confuse the claiming process by introducing an additional person for the adoptive parents to acknowledge and be grateful to. In his book *The Children* deHartog has written, "The haunting thought of the unknown woman is the most formidable obstacle the mother will have to overcome before she can fully convince herself of the validity of her own motherhood."[1] With foster caretakers, the child has not just a set of birthparents who have influenced him, but another set of two nurturers as well. Since many adoptive parents initially follow a pattern of trying to deny some of adoption's differences, it is possible for them to subconsciously refuse to acknowledge the existence of unknown birthparents by transferring their acknowledgement feelings to fosterparents whom they are likely to have met and can afford to have continued contact with since the foster caretakers represent no real "threat" to them in that they have no possible claim on the child.

For the benefit of children, who deserve the continuity of

one set of nurturing parents, foster care should be avoided whenever possible and should never be a routine part of agency practice, as it impedes the claiming process by hampering the parents' ability to establish their own parenting style.

Because adoption is so definitely different from parenting by birth, successful parenting in adoption is never as straightforwardly "easy" and "natural" as is giving birth. There are too many complicating factors in an adoption for an adoptor to assume that adoption of a healthy infant will be "just like" giving birth.

Having considered the tasks to accomplish in successfully building a sense of entitlement and claiming a particular child as their own, how might we know, either as preadoptive or adoptive parents or as professionals working with such couples, that this process is successfully progressing? How do we know that a couple is resolving their infertility, has accepted adoption's differences from biological parenting to the extent that they are consistently able to acknowledge these differences in their parenting, and have learned to deal successfully with the negative feelings about adoption expressed by outsiders?

In discussing clues to a poorly developing sense of entitlement we need to recognize that the issues will be uncomfortable to some because they will seem "threatening." So normal are these behaviors that most adoptive parents can remember a time when each of these "symptoms" was a part of their own thinking and behavior. In fact, for some considering them now, these attitudes and behaviors may be current. Does this mean that these people are not potentially good adoptive parents? Not necessarily. One of the most important things for one to realize is that resolution of infertility and building a sense of entitlement are both processes of growth. Time and education will change attitudes toward infertility and adoption a number of times over the course of any person's life. The people we are today are not the people we will become in five years any more than we are now the people we were five years ago.

What, then, might indicate that a family needs assistance in developing a sense of entitlement?

1. Prolonged denial of any feelings of disappointment about one's inability to parent biologically or denial that one has come to adoption out of necessity rather than as a first choice in family building.

2. Persistent fantasies about what might have been with the biological children who do not exist.

3. Strong resentment of a particular social worker or of agency involvement in general, or perhaps a decision to use private adoption for the purpose of avoiding a pre-placement home study. (Since there are many other reasons for using the option of private adoption, it is important that this not be construed as a general problem for all couples pursuing this option.)

4. A reluctance to discuss the fact of adoption at all with non-family members to the extent of trying to keep the fact of adoption a secret.

5. Conversely, an obsession with discussing adoption at any and all opportunities, many of which are entirely inappropriate.

6. Obsessive fears that a child to be adopted will not measure up to family standards. This can take many forms, from a strong need to have a child physically match the family, to unrealistic worries about the birth-parents' lifestyles and basic intelligence which results in a set of unreasonably positive or negative expectations for the child. The September, 1983, issue of *OURS Magazine* contained an interesting article called "Wanted: an E.R.A. (Equal Rights in Adoption) for Boys," which discussed the large discrepancy between a desire for boys among first time expectant biological

parents (80% of whom consistently indicate a wish for a first born boy) and the consistency with which 54% of first time adoptive parents prefer to adopt a girl. These preferences have been well documented in both biologically and adoptively build families and trends continue today. Female infants continue to be preferred by today's adopting couples and, among waiting children, the number of girls who remain unplaced is much smaller than the number of boys. Among families who have already given birth to children the same prejudice applies. Families are willing to come to adoption in order to add a girl to their families after having given birth to several boys in succession, but many fewer families are willing to adopt a son after the birth of several girls. The authors of this article theorize that the adoption of a girl satisfies the mother's maternal nurturing role without threatening a father's paternal responsibilities for continuing his bloodline through a male child.

7. Uncomfortable attitudes about the child's birthparents and fears of the possibility of search. Sometimes this manifests itself in a need to compete with the birthparents or to deny the importance of birthparents in the child's life. In some cases parents find the adoption of a foreign born child of interest because it so effectively cuts off the possibility of later contact with the birthfamily.

8. Anxiety about discussing the adoption with the child. It is perfectly normal to become anxious about this as parents wait for a child adopted as an infant to begin to ask questions on his own.. After all, "The Telling" is one of the milestones of adoptive parenting. However, when this anxiety continues so that each time it is brought up by the child the parent becomes nervous, anxious, perhaps tearful and tries to delay the discussion or is unwilling to openly respond to the child's

questions, the behavior indicates a problem.

9. The inability to discipline consistently and effectively, which may come from a fear that the child won't love a strict parent or from damaged self-esteem which allows a parent to believe that they are not deserving of the realness of parenthood with all its responsibilities, or from guilty feelings a parent may have about his child's inability to encounter his genetic past. As a group traditional adoptors often feel very guilty about disciplining their children, chastising themselves for their occasional strongly negative feelings toward their children because they believe that it is abnormal to feel so negatively about a child they wanted so desparately and worked so hard to get.

10. Discomfort with a teen adoptee's developing sexuality which may come to a parent whose own sexual identity has been damaged by unresolved infertility issues.

Our feelings of inadequacy about ourselves as people can affect our feelings of adequacy as parents. Doubts about our own adequacy and the realness of the family relationship will be perceived by a child, as well, since children tend to respond more readily to the nuances of communication than they do to the actual words they hear. A child's perception of himself as a whole and healthy human being and his own acceptance of the realness of his family will suffer if his parents are not feeling confident and competent in their relationship with him.

Parents by adoption and the professionals who work with them must understand that sometimes parents may need to sink back into behavior which rejects adoption's differences. These occasional lapses are perfectly normal. They should, however, be recognized by the parent as something to work on. Infertility, after all, hurts. Consistent challenges to the authenticity of our families by the public hurts, too. Adoption is not the same as parenting by giving birth, and adoption brings with it a unique blend of gains and losses, happiness and pain for each of those whom it touches. Denial of these facts does not improve the situation, but can make it worse.

Time is a factor in the healing process of resolution and in developing a sense of entitlement, so that the question becomes just what should be expected of an infertile couple pursuing the adoption alternative? How "resolved" need they be on the day they put their names on a list awaiting a homestudy? How resolved need they be when the home-study begins? How "entitled" must they feel on the day that a child is finally placed in their home? How much more entitled must they be by the time a preschooler asks, "Mommy, Johnny says there's a baby in his Mommy's tummy. Did I grown in your tummy?"

My answer is to repeat that resolution of infertility and entitlement building in adoption are processes of growth. A couple should not expect of themselves that on the day they phone the agency to inquire about adoption they would be ready to take a newborn home with them and welcome a visit from his birthparents for tea. Although there will be some prospective adoptive parents for whom this really feels like a good idea, most will not think so.

Instead, I would suggest that a phone call to an agency could be made while the couple is still in the process of working on a possible pregnancy, assuming that this couple has examined their feelings about the losses of a biologically connected child and the pregnancy experience and feels that the loss of the possibility of parenting is more important to them. The wait for a homestudy is usually lengthy. As well, many agencies accept couples only when their ages fall beneath a certain limit at the time of application. It is easier to remove a name from a list than it is to get it on one. While waiting for the homestudy to begin, prospective adoptive parents should be encouraged to complete remaining fertility testing or treatment, to read about adoption, to speak with adoptive parents, to learn something about adoption-interested groups and to become involved in them, and to attend adoption seminars.

Prospective adoptors should not expect of themselves that at the time they put their names on what they know to be a lengthy waiting list they need to have fully committed themselves to the adoption alternative. By the time the homestudy begins, however, assuming that they have been given assurances by the agency that the homestudy process is one of education and preparation rather than a screening out process, and if the agency's policy is that a placement should occur within a year of the approval process, prospective adoptive parents should be ready to commit much of their energy to preparation for adoption in much the same way as they would devote themselves to preparing for birth were they pregnant.

At some point during the homestudy process an agency is likely to suggest that it is important that a couple stop all medical treatments for infertility. "Normal infertile" couples, who have found no medical reason for their inability to conceive, are sometimes asked to use birth control during the period from approval for adoption through placement and finalization. Most infertile couples find this request both threatening and unreasonable. This reaction comes as a result of their inability to believe that a baby will really be forthcoming and as a continuation of the attitude often acquired during their frustrating race to become parents that they must push in all directions ceaselessly without stopping to pause, rest and reflect.

It is important that adoption workers understand that infertile couples often have become overly wary about trusting that the professionals with whom they work can actually help them to become parents. Just as physicians often promised them that they would become pregnant with just one more demanding treatment or procedure which was ultimately unsuccessful, adoption workers now promise that they will become parents if they submit to what the couple may perceive as the indignities of a homestudy . . . but only if they agree to burn their remaining bridges to biological parenthood. Such a request is often seen by the pre-adoptive couple as an arbitrary exercise of control by a god-like agency which further strips them of their own control over their family planning. In order to agree to such a demand without having been carefully educated about the reasons for it, couples would have to make a leap of faith that is nearly impossible.

Is it, then, important that pre-adoptive couples stop treatment and/or practice birth control while actively involved in the adoption process? Expectant biological parents have nine months to prepare for the arrival of their child. During this time they introspectively fantasize, communicate with one another in joint fantasy while sharing common fears and anxieties, and they begin the practical steps of nest-building: creating physical and emotional space for the new phase in their lives as they grow to love the particular child with whom they are pregnant. They experience a series of developmental stages which have been identified as:

1. Pregnancy Validation —accepting the pregnancy as a reality.

2. Fetal Embodiment —incorporating the fetus into the mother's body image.

3. Fetal Distinction —seeing the fetus as a separate entity in order to make plans for him.

4. Role Transition —preparing to take on the parenting role. [2]

They are encouraged to follow their own progress through these stages.

Adoptive parents, too, need this psychological preparation for parenthood. When couples are allowed and encouraged to invest emotional energy in such preparation, the attachment process between parents and child —the entitlement process so vital to successful adoptive parenting —will be enhanced. In fact, it is theorized that well prepared pre-adoptive couples will experience their own stages of preparation for parenthood:

1. Adoption Validation —accepting the fact that their child will join the family by adoption rather than by birth.

2. Child Embodiment —incorporating the child by adoption into the parents' emotional images.

3. Child Distinction —beginning to perceive of the child as a reality in order to make plans for him.

4. Role Transition —preparing to take on the parenting in adoption role. [3]

Pre-adoptive couples should be educated about the need for this process. They need to understand that psychological preparation for parenting in adoption cannot be accomplished successfully during a period when much of their emotional and physical energy and financial resources are being put into the consuming tasks of temperature graphs, treatments, scheduled intercourse, more treatments, and the two week cycles of hope and despair which accompany infertility treatment. By the time an agency makes such a request of a couple, then, it is important that they have completed the grieving process for the child of their assumptions and have come to see themselves as whole human beings with a relationship strengthened by their having faced what may have been their first major life crisis. This will allow them to use the weeks and months of the homestudy and the subsequent wait for placement for more positive growth.

During this period couples should work toward a goal of learning about and accepting adoptive parenting's differences from biological parenthood, finding ways to acquire needed child care skills, and moving out of infertility's isolation to reestablish potential family support systems. Ideally they should be encouraged to attend preparation for parenting classes specifically designed for adoptive parents-to-be. Such classes will help couples to acquire needed skills, will help them to find ways to prepare their own families for the coming child (a child which does not match his grandparents' and aunts' and uncles' assumptions any better than he does his parents'), and will provide an opportunity outside of the homestudy for couples to explore their questions and fears. Such classes may be offered in any community by a RESOLVE chapter, by an adoptive parents' group, by hospital parent education programs, by the Red Cross, etc. If they are not available yet in your community, you may wish to encourage their implementation. A thorough curriculum guide for such a series has been developed —*Our Child: Preparation For Parenting In Adoption - Instructor's Guide,* by Carol A. Hallenbeck B.S., R.N., a 233 page course complete with a wealth of resources and a thorough bibliography. (See resources section for ordering information.)

Even with such careful preparation it should not be assumed that at the point of placement infertility will no longer be painful. As a matter of fact, infertility is often particularly painful during the first weeks after a child's arrival. At no other time will an adoptive couple hear such a concentration of comments about the adoption. In particular, as they adjust to the exhaustion that the arrival of a new child in any house brings, they will be very aware of just how chauvinistic their friends and family are about the birth experience. New parents by birth are expected to be tired, to take leaves of absence from work and volunteer commitments. Food is brought in and there are countless offers of household help while the new mother rests from the experience of birth. New adoptive parents have the same adjustments to make and the same lack of sleep as do new biological parents. However, visitors tend to forget this and to assume that the new parents will act as hosts. They tend to make new parents feel like Cinderella, alone in the kitchen while everyone else enjoys the new baby. This, too, shall pass. And, as the sense of entitlement grows and the new family settles into a routine, days will go by when the couple does not think about the fact of adoption at all.

Will infertility's pain ever come back? Yes. It may become particularly acute once more when the couple is frustrated in trying to expand their family. But eventually it will become a bittersweet twinge akin to the arthritic ache felt in a once broken bone when soggy weather sets in.

Could considering going back into medical treatment for a second or third child indicate poor resolution or lack of acceptance of the child by adoption? No. The medical possibilities in infertility are changing so rapidly from day to day that it is perfectly logical to expect that it may indeed be easier for some couples to give birth to subsequent children than to adopt them.

One of the wonderful things about the growth process of resolution and entitlement is that they often help us to become much broader people than we were before. Evolving resolution and entitlement often mean that a second child for a couple who once waited for the fabled Gerber baby may be older or handicapped or racially different from his adoptive parents . . . and not because the family feels that this was the best that they could do in a rapidly changing world of adoption, but because they have grown to see this as a first choice in expanding their family.

Helen Keller wrote these beautiful words which are meaningful in a number of ways when applied to the adoption experience:

> When one door of happiness closes, another opens. But often we look so long at the closed door that we do not see the one that has opened for us. We must all find these open doors, and if we believe in ourselves we will find them, and make ourselves and our lives as beautiful as God intended.

---

1. deHartog, Jan, *The Children: A Personal Record for the Use of Adoptive Parents.* New York: Atheneum, 1969, p. 233.

2. Floyd, Cathy, R.N., *"Pregnancy after Reproductive Failure,"* American Journal of Nursing.

3. Hallenbeck, Carol A., *Our Child: Preparation for Parenting in Adoption - Instructor's Guide.* Wayne, PA: Our Child Press, 1984, p. 24.

CHAPTER 7

THE HOMESTUDY

What constitutes an appropriate homestudy for a couple interested in expanding their family by adoption? Standardization of this process is virtually nonexistent in the adoption community. While some agencies prefer a number of private interviews with couples, who may never meet another couple involved in the process at the same agency, other agencies use group work in addition to private interviews. When groups are used, whether or not group education and interaction occurs both before and after placement or just before varies considerably from agency to agency. The extent of autobiographical data collected and in what form (i.e., letter, questionnaire, etc.) also is dependent upon who does the homestudy and for what purpose. Some agencies use psychological testing and/or values clarification instruments, while others rely solely on the subjective impressions of their professionals. While few couples have met the mythical white gloved inspector who examines homes, there is considerable variation as to what constitutes a home visit, from the complete tour of house and yard by a worker who throws in child proofing suggestions as well, to the visit from a worker who spends ten minutes perched on the living room chair closest to the front door, evidently satisfied just to confirm that there indeed is an occupied dwelling at the address provided.

While it is difficult to suggest that standardization would improve the homestudy process, it is important that agencies realize that the large variations from agency to agency are part of what widens the credibility gap between adoptors and professionals. If a step is important at one agency, why is it left out at another? If one agency feels it unnecessary to require a certain procedure, why is the other so adamant about requiring it?

Rarely do adoptors feel confident enough in their "approvability" to openly question the process. Increasingly, however, prospective adoptors are approaching the adoption-interested groups in which they are involved to request group advocacy, which serves to raise the issues while both protecting the anonymity of the concerned party as well as bolstering the complaint's apparent validity through the sheer numbers of a group of any size.

Among the homestudy issues being questioned are these:

Psychological Testing

Increasingly agencies are using psychological testing as a screening tool within their homestudy process. While in principle the use of such a device has merit, as it is used in practice there are several reasons that clients react negatively to the idea.

First, agencies often do not have a clearly defined policy delineating their reasons for such testing and defining how results are to be used. Clients are not well prepared for the testing, then, in that they do not clearly understand how the results will be evaluated and by whom, how the results will be used in determining their approval or disapproval for a placement, and what follow up might be suggested should the reported results reflect poorly upon them.

Second, the instrument used most often is one developed during the 1940's. Many adoptors question whether such a test, with sexist overtones and forty year old values as a base, can possibly be currently accurate. Almost never is an agency representative prepared to address these issues backed up by expertise in the field of psychological testing.

Third, couples often are concerned about the fact that such tests become part of a permanent record. Agencies need to address the issue of just who will have access to such test results, how long the information will be retained, and under what circumstances and to whom it could conceivably be released.

Fourth, many couples who adopt more than once find themselves repeating this test each time they adopt. Without the careful preparation that could be done by one expert in the application of psychological testing, couples often question the value of repeating this same test and do not receive satisfactory answers. They may then become increasingly resentful of what they may perceive as a waste of their time and the needless expenditure of the money spent to score these relatively expensive tools.

At least one couple interviewed for this section related the story of one partner's negative test results, with which they strongly disagreed. Though the test results clearly suggested that this person was an unlikely prospect for approval, this couple was approved, as the caseworker chose simply to disregard this negative material, apparently on the basis of personal knowledge of the couple. No confirming test was administered, nor was a suggestion made that the person be screened by a psychologist. This couple had a number of concerns about this situation. Certainly if the results of such testing are important to the evaluation process for adoptive couples and if their revelations can be trusted, a willingness to disregard their results in some instances and to make negative decisions based upon them in others does not appear to follow good social work practice. As well, with no follow up of any kind to either confirm or deny the results of this testing, this person was concerned about the test's remaining a part of a permanent record.

Certainly if such tests are to become a standard part of any agency's homestudy process, the agency should establish specific policies regarding their use and application. To prevent misinterpretation and misunderstanding, it is recommended that such policies be put in writing, so that couples can read and reread them, ask appropriate questions, and be referred to them. This written information might best include a thorough discussion of the strengths and weaknesses of the instrument being used, a statement of what the results will and will not be used for, and a route of appeal should applicants strongly disagree with the results of their testing. Above all, agencies who do choose to administer such testing should do so consistently, and clients should be able to expect that their results will be used consistently.

References

The need to provide references is for many adoptors one of the most uncomfortable aspects of the homestudy. Numbers and types of references required vary considerably among agencies, as does the form in which they are to be submitted. References from some or all of the following may be requested: prospective grandparents, aunts and uncles; employers; friends; neighbors; clergypersons; the school of other children within the family.

The need to supply references destroys completely and forever any privacy the prospective parents may have had concerning their family building plans. While couples contemplating becoming pregnant need never make this known to friends, family, employer, etc. until they are successful in their efforts, the reference gathering aspect of the adoption process requires that adoptors ask for the co-operation of others in gaining agency approval. Buried in the discomfort of asking for such a reference is the adoptor's fear that he may indeed be rejected by the agency and then be placed in the position of having to explain this to those who supplied references.

It can be humiliating to ask for references for such a purpose, as it may seem as if one is requesting permission to take what for others is a totally natural and independent action —building a family. This factor enhances the adoptor's feelings of being out of control. After all, what prospective parent by birth must depend upon the positive reactions to themselves and their family plans from parents, neighbors, employers, etc., in order to add a child to their family?

The format in which references are supplied can also be of concern. Some agencies request general letters of reference with few if any specific guidelines, while others supply a highly detailed questionnaire to be filled out. Most often there has been no attempt to design individual reference models for each type of reference supplier, so that the adoptor is placed in the awkward position of asking people to supply information about which the referor may not have knowledge.

Most of those asked to supply references are not comfortable doing so. Aware that they themselves have not needed such public permission to parent, they feel awkward. But, when information is requested to which they feel that they cannot or should not appropriately respond, they feel the weight of responsibility given over to them by the person needing the reference, and, to a certain extent intimidated by the authority of the system, they would be hesitant to question the agency's procedure and thereby risk jeopardizing the adoptor's chances.

This area of references is another in which specific written policy should be available to adoptors. What does the agency hope to learn from each type of reference requested? Have they made that clear by designing tools specifically for each type of referor? What will be the agency's reaction to a questionable reference or an entirely negative one? Is a system of checks and balances in place that will guarantee the adoptors the opportunity to defend themselves while at the same time protecting the confidentiality of the referor? When references are well justified and carefully developed tools are used, couples will be somewhat less resentful of their need to supply them.

Supervision

The supervisory period between placement and finalization varies in length from a few weeks to a year or more. Most agencies depend almost exclusively on preplacement interviews and education to assure themselves that adoptive families have been well prepared for adoption. While more and more agencies are making effective use of group work in the homestudy process, providing education and interaction to several prospective adoptors at one time and thus not only making more efficient use of worker time but also providing a peer interaction which is intended to and often does evolve into an effective support system for the expanding families who work together, in almost all cases this education and formal group work is expected to be accomplished before placement.

Postplacement agency/family interaction, then, most often consists of a minimal number of contacts —less than a handful of phone calls and one or two breezy and almost superficial home visits before finalization of the adoption is accomplished. The group work and education provided before the placement dealt in theory. Adoptors were presented with a series of "What if's" about which to speculate. Now that parenthood is **real,** new parents face the practical aspects of raising a child. Still, at no other time are the parents of an infant less likely to confess their ambivalent feelings to their social worker than during supervision. Parenthood is now **real,** not the fantasy held onto for years; and a child is now **real** and loved. Who could imagine losing the baby now! Isolated again in their one on one relationship with a "powerful" caseworker, most adoptors do a kind of psychological holding of their breaths until a gavel pounds and adoption proceedings are pronounced final.

Several agencies, groups, and adoption-focused professionals across the country who work particularly within the area of special needs placement have recognized the need for follow-up and even long term on-going services to adoption-built families. Though most likely couples adopting a healthy infant would not need such intensive services (some of these programs build in the expectation of a need for individual and family therapy) perhaps the recognition that the practical nature of real parenting makes adoptors more likely to absorb needed information than does theory presented during their fantasizing should encourage agencies to consider inverting their programs, providing more attention during the supervisory period and encouraging more self-education, group involvement, and participation in conferences and classes during the preplacement period.

Updates

Those paying attention to the needs of children in the U.S. and the world over will have been exposed repeatedly to a most upsetting statistic: more than 100,000 U.S. children languish in the limbo of foster care and over half of them are legally free and waiting for homes. Experienced adoptors are not surprised when they hear the complaints of would-be first time adoptors reacting to media publicity about a specific child that it is difficult to get a homestudy done. Often, however, they are surprised the first time they find themselves in the position of needing an update.

The majority of traditional and preferential adoptors who adopt once at least consider adopting again. Usually their expectation is that a subsequent adoption will be easier than the first, in that, having proven themselves capable as adoptive parents, they will find the homestudy update less complicated and more comfortable than their original homestudy. Sometimes adoptors are fortunate enough to find that the agency and the worker who completed their first study are willing to provide this service and assist them with another placement, so that the process truly does involve a gathering of updated materials and a reacquaintance with a family already known to the agency. But because we live in a highly mobile society, either worker or adoptor are likely to have moved on before an update can be completed at the original agency. Sometimes, too, agencies "specialize" in a particular kind of adoption —infant, foreign, American special needs —and will not be prepared to update a homestudy should a family expand their horizons in a subsequent adoption.

Most reasonable people would agree that a family wishing to experience a different style of adoption from their first (e.g., the adoptor of a healthy white infant considering an older child or a foreign infant or a transracial placement) needs new education specifically designed to meet the needs of that adoption alternative and needs to examine once again their motivations and expectations about the placement. Too often, however, even couples wishing to repeat the kind of adoption they experienced before find themselves faced with the need to begin completely from scratch if they wish to adopt again. Without professional uniformity in the home study process, many adoption professionals are unwilling to accept the work done by another professional. So, in the interests of being conscientious and thorough, they insist on the adoptors' repeating the process of references, psychological testing, group work, etc., rather than "compromise" their own standards.

Increasingly special needs adoption demands the cooperation of two agencies in approving a placement and completing an adoption —a custodial agency in one city who holds parental authority for the child, and an agency in the prospective parents' city willing to do the supervision of the adoption. The unwillingness of the supervisory agency to accept the requirements of the placing agency causes needless irritation and red tape for all involved and sometimes even jeopardizes a placement for a waiting child.

Such an attitude that "we do it better than they do" not only insults other agencies directly, but adds to the anxiety of adoptors, who not only find themselves with no more control than they had before even though they've gained considerable confidence but also receive the unspoken message that perhaps they aren't really "approvable" by this second agency. This lack of respect for the work of "competing" professionals and/or institutions also adds to the public's impression of the adoption system as unorganized, unstandardized, needlessly competitive and inefficiently duplicative.

Money Matters

Many public agencies don't charge fees at all. All private agencies do, but the size of the fee and the method by which it is determined vary considerably. Fees may be based on a flat across-the-board sum for all adoptors, on direct costs of services, or on a percentage of income with or without a ceiling. At some agencies flat fees include everything from the homestudy through the legal costs of finalization. At other agencies each service is paid for piecemeal, beginning with an application fee and following up with a specific fee for each counseling session or group workshop.

Allocation of funds collected from placement fees varies considerably from agency to agency as well. At some agencies fees become part of a general fund paying all expenses of the agency's many services. At other agencies adoption fees remain exclusively in the adoption program. As well, some agencies further divide their program so that funds collected from adoption fees are not applied to expenses incurred in providing services to birthparents who do not make adoption plans. More commonly, services to the over 90% of birthparents who do not make adoption plans are paid for from the fees collected from adoptors.

Perhaps no aspect of the relationship between prospective adoptors and the agencies with whom they work is more uniformly uncomfortable for everyone involved than is the issue of finances. Caseworkers don't like to talk about it, often to the extent that they gloss over this topic in their discussions with families so that misunderstandings may occur. Families don't like to think about it, as it points out another way in which they are singled out as very different from families formed by birth. Agency directors are almost always people firmly committed to human services, so that they care very much about the negative impact of fees on their clients, but then again, fees are their programs' life's blood.

There is rampant schizophrenia in the rhetoric that accompanies a discussion of fees. Agencies are highly offended at the mention of the word "purchase" when applied to the placement of a baby, yet it is still the case that only healthy, white infants command full fees.

Public agencies usually handle both infant adoptions and the adoption of older children. Most often private agencies specialize in the placement of infants and occasionally have custodial responsibilities for older children, so that their involvement in special needs adoptions is usually in the role of updating a homestudy and perhaps supervising a placement for custodial agency which has determined the placement.

Rarely are infants who are handicapped or non-Caucasian placed at full fee because of the difficulty in finding families willing to pay large sums. As a result, many of the private agencies who occasionally need to make a placement of a handicapped child or an older child do so by seeking families outside of their approved and waiting list and in doing so waive the fee or drastically reduce it.

Still, when agencies are questioned about their fees they respond that adoptors must understand that there are expenses in adoption services and, since somebody must pay for them, why not adoptors who benefit most from their services? There is surface logic to this argument until several common questions are posed: How do adoptors benefit from services supplied to non-placing parents? Of course there are expenses in adoption, but no one involved in special needs adoption suggests that adopting families should reimburse custodial agencies for several years of counseling and foster care in making these placements, so at what age do children cease to become worth paying for? How is it logical that a percentage of income is a "fair" assessment as a placement fee when parents by birth do not pay in this manner?

Few adoptors would argue that someone has to pay for services. Few would argue that direct services provided to them and their family should be paid for by them. There is seldom an argument about whether or not adoptors should pay for their own counseling time, their own psychological testing, and most would extend this same logic to include their assuming their own child's birthparents' counseling fees and medical expenses. Many adoptors come to their personal limits when asked to carry the financial burden for children not placed for adoption or for placements other than their own.

This adoptor's advocate would suggest that direct expenses involved in a particular placement are the only legitimate fees which should be passed along to an adoptor, and that agencies should spearhead an effort to lobby for changes in medical insurance that would allow for reimbursement to adopting families for medical expenses incurred with the pregnancy and birth of a child legally adopted by the family and/or changes in tax policies that would make adoption-related expenses tax deductible as are expenses related to the arrival of a child by birth.

The problem still comes down to some very basic questions. What constitutes a legitimate fee and where does babyselling begin? (Agencies must be aware that a desperate childless couple will have a very difficult time understanding how a licensed agency could charge them $14,000 for the placement of an infant and still be considered legitimate when they are able to arrange for a private adoption that many adoption professionals would consider "babyselling" at less than one third that sum.) If we believe in the value of all life, how can we allow healthy babies to be more "valuable" than unhealthy ones or than older children? Just who should be responsible for the rising tide of costs related to unplanned pregnancies in this country? These are issues that must be faced squarely and addressed by all who care about adoption.

In some ways, then, wide variations in the manner in which homestudies are done have widened the credibility gap between adoptors and professionals. In order to work toward closing this gap, agencies must consider reevaluating their policies and offering their clients carefully written explanations of and justifications for their homestudy procedures. Such information will best be received when it anticipates many of the unspoken hesitancies adoptors hold and nips in the bud misunderstandings about how the process will be handled.

CHAPTER 8

TRADITIONAL ADOPTORS AND WAITING CHILDREN

The relationship between agency and adoptor has changed as the face of adoption has changed over the last three decades. Once agencies existed to find "blue ribbon" babies for "Barbie and Ken" couples. Orphanages existed for unhealthy or racially "undesirable" infants. Children who came into the system beyond infancy were considered un-adoptable. There was an abundance of healthy babies because adoption was then seen as the only acceptable option for dealing with an untimely pregnancy. Agency requirements were less stringent than they are today because there were more babies to adopt than there were families to adopt them. Often couples were allowed to view and select from two or more healthy babies. Though treatments for infertility were more difficult a generation ago, a solution to childlessness was easier. Couples who lost control of their fertility regained control of the family planning aspect of their lives by actually "choosing" their child.

Today there are still more children to adopt than there are potential parents asking for them. But those children aren't healthy babies. They are older, handicapped, racially different than the majority of adoptors, and in sibling groups. These children have entered today's adoption system for a variety of reasons, many of which didn't even exist a generation ago. Waiting children exist in large numbers, and in the last several years child advocates have done an admirable job of changing professional attitudes about such children who were once seen as unadoptable and shuffled off to institutions with little attempt to find adoptive families for them, so that now, permanency is the goal for every child, and caseworkers are pressured to find these children homes.

Since infertile couples have always made up the primary

pool of potential adoptors, it is logical that adoption workers' first thoughts turn to these couples when they ponder who will parent waiting children. Many infertile couples are interested in this option and do adopt special needs children quite successfully. However, many other infertile couples are uncomfortable with the thought of raising children they will not have an opportunity to parent from birth or children who are racially different than themselves. While they feel that they would have accepted a child born to them with a severe handicap, they are not comfortable in making a deliberate choice to parent a handicapped child. These attitudes come from their assumptions, and those of most of society, that parenting is easier when you do it "from scratch."

There is one main reason for the inability of many infertile couples to make the transition from traditional adoptor to preferential adoptor to consider special needs adoption. They are **normal** people. Like everyone else they have fears, doubts, and prejudices. As a group they have the same needs, dreams, and values as do fertile couples. Proportionately, then, they are no more likely to see special needs adoption as a family building method of choice than are their fertile counterparts.

Parenting is never easy, but it becomes more difficult when the baggage of several years spent with other families, racial differences, or profound handicaps is added to it. This is the primary reason that the vast majority of parents considering family expansion prefer to do so by giving birth over and over again rather than by adopting children already born and in need of homes. All of society accept this reasoning on the part of fertile couples and do not think poorly of them when they choose not to adopt. A value system exists that declares that birth is superior to adoption as a method of family planning. Most people, then, are delighted but somewhat surprised by the fertile couple who chooses to adopt rather than to give birth to some of their children and tend to heap praise and admiration on such adoptors on the one hand ("Aren't you people wonderful to take that child! I don't know how you do it. I don't think I could, but I'm sure glad that there are people out there like you!") and on the other hand view the motivations of such couples as somewhat suspect ("Why would you want to take someone else's reject? You're asking for trouble!")

Social workers share the same value system held by the majority of society, thus many of them have become increasingly intolerant of infertile couples who do not seek out waiting children. Frustrated by the need to find homes for children in need of them and faced with increasing numbers of potential adoptors inquiring about the almost nonexistent "Gerber baby," adoption workers wish that the ideal could be met: that children in need of homes and couples who want children could meet each other's needs. Faced with this practical crisis, adoption workers often subconsciously buy into that old adage "Beggars can't be choosers" as they consider infertile couples in the adoption approval process. "If you really wanted a child," comes the message (not just from the uninformed neighbor but from the social work professional, too), "you'd take one of those homeless kids they advertise in the papers."

Thus a double standard which has always been at work in society at large has filtered down to the social work professional. An adoption worker who would not judge negatively a fertile couple's decision to give birth rather than to adopt an older child reacts impatiently toward and even questions the motivations for parenthood of the infertile couple seeking a healthy infant. The existence of this double standard further widens the credibility gap between adoption professionals and traditional adoptors.

In addition to the fact that they are normal and thus no more inclined to see special needs adoption as a family building method of choice than is the average fertile couple, there are a number of logical reasons why many childless infertile couples are initially unable to see themselves as parents of a waiting child.

Infertility, as we have discussed, often is damaging to the self-esteem. Not having had the opportunity to parent by the traditional method, infertile couples often hold the unexpressed fear that they will be unable to do a good job, perhaps even feeling that "Somebody up there might have been trying to tell us something when He made us infertile. Maybe we should listen." They desperately want to get as close to the "real" experience as they can in order to test their fitness for parenting. Children with special problems, such couples feel, need special parenting skills that they question whether they have the ability to acquire.

Often, however, the infertile couple who has once or twice experienced parenting a healthy infant will have gained enough confidence in their parenting abilities to feel good about a special needs placement in further expanding their family. With this decision they move from the status of traditional adoptor to that of preferential adoptor. Ironically, however, such couples often do not have the opportunity to adopt a waiting child, since in far too many agencies placements are done on the basis of how efficiently they can be handled for the professionals. It is much easier to place a tenth child in a family that has already proven themselves good at special needs placements than it is to go through the education process with someone new to the experience. So, when the infertile couple finds themselves waiting for a homestudy with a professional who is far too busy to begin one again and at the same time they watch other families (often mixed "bio" and adoptive families of amazing size who have become local legends in the adoption community) simply make a phone call to get another placement or in fact to be called upon by an agency "in urgent need" of a home for a child, they once again begin to experience feelings of self doubt. Eventually they may give up and remove themselves from the waiting list.

Another reason that infertile couples are frequently unable to see themselves as potential adoptors of waiting children is the often buried feeling that they are being treated as "second class citizens" offered what society sees as "second rate goods" rejected by everyone else but seen as "all that they can get" or "all they deserve." This too-negative-to-voice feeling is inextricably tied up in the traditional adoptor's feelings of powerlessness; but it is being fed by the approach to special needs adoption taken by most agencies. Special needs adoption is generally faster than infant adoption; there are fewer requirements and qualifications to meet; agency fees are often lower or nonexistent; subsidies sometimes exist which appear to "pay" people to accept such children. To the couple looking from the outside, not able even to get close enough to the realities of special needs adoption to be properly educated, and thus primed to misinterpret what little they do know, such facts and fantasies are frightening and even demeaning.

Third, adoption is often difficult for extended families to accept in principle. Couples sometimes feel that they have let their families down with their infertility, fear being rejected by them, and they feel that a baby of their own race might more easily be accepted by their families, allowing both themselves and their children to experience the "realness" of multigenerational family dynamics that they might miss out on if their family did not accept a special needs adoptee.

Some social workers, family counselors, and mental health professionals have also expressed reasons for feeling that on the whole childless infertile couples are not the best group from which to recruit parents for waiting children. Some of those reasons reflect the acknowledgment of infertile couples' own hesitancy about this option. Special needs adoptions are statistically more likely to disrupt than are infant adoptions. Reasons for these adoption disruptions include poor preparation of both adoptive parents and adoptees which is often aggravated by unrealistic expectations on the part of adoptee, social worker and adoptive parents. Lack of parental experience can often be responsible for unrealistic expectations. One who has had no experience in "normal" family-setting behavior for a particular childhood age can have a very difficult time sorting out what behavior is peculiar to the age of a child, what is related to the damage in his past, and what is associated with his present family situation. As well, one who has not had experience in parenting before is not as likely as an experienced parent to have full confidence in his or her own ability to parent and to exercise consistency in parenting.

These concerns are controversial. They should not be generalized to allow the assumption that no infertile childless couples would make good adoptive parents for a waiting child. They are presented instead to make a broader point. While the purpose of adoption is to provide permanent homes for children in need of them, rather than to provide children for infertile couples, it remains that there are three large groups of clients served by child placement agencies: birthfamilies, children in need of adoption, and infertile couples. Just as social service agencies are coming to see that the needs of birthparents dealing with an unplanned pregnancy and infertile couples seeking a baby are not necessarily solved by one another, in that well over 90% of the birthparents that child placement agencies now work with choose not to make adoption plans for their children, it is important that agencies come to see that the unmet needs of children waiting for homes and those of infertile couples will not necessarily match. The needs of infertile couples, birthfamilies, and waiting children are not necessarily pieces of one puzzle waiting to be completed by an adoption professional. Instead, the needs of each client group must be addressed separately and programs designed to meet each group's unique needs. In many cases, perhaps even in the majority of cases, the solutions to the needs of each of these client groups will not overlap.

What is to be done, then, about the waiting children? Better personal education about special needs adoption with those already considering adoption and broad public education of those who are not are the best answers. There are many families out there both fertile and infertile who could be educated to consider expanding their families by adoption. But of course, fertile couples are even less likely to become interested in adoption until the process of adoption is modified to become positive and responsive to individual adoptors' needs rather than restrictive and judgemental. As well, with each new political administration the focus on adoption needs shifts. Those who care about adoption need to become political advocates for children as well as social advocates.

CHAPTER 9

STEPPING STONES —A PROGRAM FOR INFERTILE COUPLES

This book has addressed adoption issues primarily from the point of view of infertile couples. Although their needs often overlap those of preferential adoptors, in many instances the needs of these two groups are different. In particular, since working through issues related to their inability to conceive and bear a biological child is a step in the entitlement building process unique to infertile couples, some of the services offered to them must focus on this issue.

Though all helping professionals would like to be able to offer definitive services to their clients, most professionals today recognize that in a rapidly changing world where all aspects of our lives carry physical, financial, emotional and sociological ramifications this is impossible. Increasingly professionals in all of the helping fields are coming to see that networking both with other professionals and with volunteer-staffed organizations is the most efficient and effective method of assuring that clients receive all of the services that they will need.

Adoption professionals use a variety of networks in their work. However, there still remains a tendency on the part of many agencies working with adoptions to try to provide all of the services they see as important for their clients. It is important that such agencies accept that it will be next to impossible for them to offer all of the services that their families might need or desire. First, funding cutbacks have meant that agencies are in the position of eliminating services rather than adding them. Second, the inherent credibility gap between adoptors and adoption workers will work against agencies in being able to adequately provide definitive services. Third, mobility factors in modern society mean that not only are families more on the move and thus not as likely as families once were to be able to reconnect with their agencies should future problems arise, but workers are also more mobile and thus if and when families do recontact their agencies they are not likely to find a person on staff who is intimately familiar with their particular case. Last, only by including a wider spectrum of people, groups, and agencies in the pool of potential support for adoption-built families can agencies hope to enhance their credibility by broadening the base of shared opinion and practice.

An important issue to consider in designing a program for infertile couples is that from their points of view many of the best services available to them will come not from professionals, but from peers. It is often difficult for professionals to give full credit to the work that volunteers are capable of doing. As a society we tend to assign more credibility to workers who are paid and services which are purchased. Infertility and adoption oriented groups provide an amazing range of services for their members/clients using tiny budgets, kitchen table offices, and volunteer labor. Some of the best information for lay people about adoption comes from volunteer produced newsletters and educational services. *News of OURS,* for example, is a bimonthly magazine of ninety-plus pages with a subscribership of over 6,000. The Open Door Society of Massachusetts also produces a bimonthly newspaper. The vast majority of parents' groups of any size produce newsletters of some kind which appear on a regular basis and often would compare quite favorably to publications produced by paid staffs. While professionally staffed organizations put on fine conferences, several of the largest and most highly regarded conferences on infertility and adoption are planned and implemented exclusively by volunteers. For example, the 1984 Northeastern Adoption Conference of the Boston ODS was attended by 900 people. RESOLVE chapters from across the country have sponsored day long symposia on infertility attended by 100 to 400 persons each. Project Orphans Abroad in Cleveland biennially offers a two day conference on adoption attended by 500. The American Adoption Conference draws people from all over the country to its four day conventions planned and offered by volunteers. The 1984 Conference of the North American Council on Adoptable Children was attended by over 1000 people and would have been impossible without primarily volunteer planning. Coalitions such as Fort Wayne, Indiana's, Adoption Forum produce programs aimed at all sides of the adoption triangle and draw 400 persons in a community of 200,000. It is lay people who do much of the work of publicizing events like National Adoption Week and organizing letter writing campaigns to legislators. It is time to acknowledge the professionalism and the high quality of services which would not be available without volunteers and to use them more efficiently and effectively.

But, you say your agency does refer families to the groups, and it isn't your fault that they choose not to take advantage of them. Perhaps you should reevaluate your method of referral. What services do you describe or emphasize? Could it perhaps be the support offered by such groups? Please remember that denying adoption's differences is a common method of coping for some adoption-built families. In refusing to acknowledge differences they will also refuse to acknowledge a need for support. Remember how important being in control of one's life situation is to a sense of well being. Adoptors will sometimes reject adoption or infertility oriented groups while thinking, "Those groups are for people with problems. We're in control here. We can handle it. We don't need help." Support is not the issue that will best "sell" group participation. Neither is social interaction. If a family is denying differences or refusing to identify with others in their same situation they will not be interested in singling themselves out by socializing with other families which are "outside the norm."

Nearly all new parents are information-hungry. Because they want to be the best parents possible, they want to know about parenting methods, about programs of benefit to parents, about books to read and to share. Often, too, adoptive couples want to keep in touch with new developments which may have an impact on their interest in expanding their adoption-built families. Parent groups are especially strong at gathering and disseminating such information. If professionals wish to encourage families to participate in parent groups, perhaps it is this benefit of group participation that should be stressed, allowing parents to discover for themselves the benefits of group support.

Perhaps the best method of encouraging group participation is to plug into the group for the couple. Physicians can subscribe to extra copies of their local chapter of RESOLVE's newsletter and give them to departing patients. They can strongly encourage attendance at symposia or a particular monthly meeting they know to be of value to a particular patient. Adoption agencies can distribute copies of adoption-oriented newsletters and encourage participation in special programs or classes almost as if they were an extension of the homestudy process. In doing so, professionals can help to prevent their patients and clients from denying the reality of their situations and encourage them to plug into helping resources beyond themselves.

A definitive program for infertile couples could quite quickly and efficiently be designed and implemented by linking services currently provided by a variety of medical, counseling and social work professionals and mutual support organizations. Such a program should begin with the patient involved in medical treatment. It might focus initially on seeking appropriate medical care, learning to evaluate services and service providers, becoming adept at serving as one's own advocate and making judgments about when to ask for a referral or a second opinion. It might include initial brief information on alternatives to biological parenting offered primarily for the purpose of helping couples to understand that some of those alternatives, such as adoption, could themselves be time consuming and difficult, so that early decision-making is important to consider.

Groups of physicians, a medical center, or a hospital might then offer, in conjunction with a RESOLVE chapter, psychologists and family counselors, a local mental health center, etc., a "when to stop" decision making program. Since today's infertility patients live in a time of ever advancing medical research with new and on the horizon treatments being announced daily, it has become increasingly difficult for them to determine when, for physical, emotional, financial, or sociological reasons, it is appropriate for them to end treatment and consider alternatives. The opportunity to work individually with a counselor should be provided for couples for whom it may seem likely that any single of the above factors or a combination of them might indicate the need to consider ending treatment.

Step three would make mandatory a six to ten week period following the end of treatment during which patients would be encouraged to work through their loss reactions either privately or in professionally facilitated peer support groups such as those successfully in use for ten years by RESOLVE chapters. This mandatory delay before continuation of alternative services would allow for normal grieving to begin and progress, a purpose which must be made very clear to couples involved in the program.

The fourth step for couples would be a decision-making workshop tailored to meet the needs of infertile couples. Merle Bombardieri's *The Baby Decision* (Rawson Wade, 1981) and Diane Elvenstar's *Children: To Have or Have Not* (Harbor, 1982) could serve as resources in developing such workshops, in which infertile couples would reexamine in light of their infertility their original decision to become parents and determine which of their three options —childfree living, adoption, semi-adoption —would be most comfortable for them to pursue. Couples deciding upon childfree living could be referred to various community projects and opportunities such as Big Brothers/Big Sisters, scouting, 4-H, church groups, etc., which would allow them to satisfy remaining needs for a limited relationship with children. They would also be referred to NON (National Organization of Non-Parents) for additional support in building a happy life among the childfree. Couples deciding upon semi-adoption (donor insemination, adoptive embryo transfer, surrogate mothering) would be referred to a sub-program of the decision-making workshops we will call here Program A, and couples considering adoption would be referred to what will be called Program B.

Program A, for patients considering the semi-adoption alternatives of donor insemination, surrogate mothering, adoptive embryo transfer, would have as its purpose providing education and assistance for couples in dealing with a variety of issues unique to such parenting options (e.g., the imbalance of "power" when one parent is the child's genetic parent and the other is not, the negative view that such an option will produce in large segments of society and how to deal with that, individual moral and religious issues that must be considered in this decision-making, the issue of sharing of facts about this conception with the child and/or family and friends, etc.) Such counseling, available both on an individual basis and with groups, would serve as a self-screening process in much the same way as many adoption home-studies now work, in that, through self-education and examination, careful communication, and cautious decision-making, couples would come to screen themselves out of the program should the process lead them to see that their motivations for considering these alternatives were inappropriate. The program would allow them to decide for themselves to proceed with this option should they find it to be a viable one for them. Those deciding to use these alternatives would them be referred to programs providing these services.

Clients considering adoption would move into Program B. The first step in this program might actually be quite useful for couples still working on their medical opportunities as well as those who have elected to stop treatment. This step would be an adoption information and decision-making series or workshop which could be patterned after the highly successful "Family Building thru Adoption" course offered throughout the state of Maryland by adoptive parent volunteers from Families Adopting Children Everywhere (see resources for ordering information.) The series would examine various adoption alternatives such as infant vs. older child, healthy vs. handicapped, same race vs. transracial, domestic vs. foreign, agency vs. private and could provide the participants with an adoption resource packet for their state for the purpose of helping them to learn about local agencies and to refer themselves to those that are appropriate to serve them in their chosen adoption alternative. If no group in your state has yet developed such a resource guide, consider asking a local infertility- or adoption-oriented group or a service group such as the Junior League to produce one. In areas where these are available they have often been developed very inexpensively using grant funds from such sources as drug companies, retail children's stores, medical societies or their auxiliaries, etc. The one for Illinois, produced by the Junior League of Chicago, is distributed free. Those for Indiana and for Utah and some other states were developed by RESOLVE chapters and are available for a small fee. An adoption exploration course such as this could most effectively be offered by an adoptive parent group or an infertility group, with an adoptive parent or parent couple as leader. At its end most couples should have had most of their preliminary concerns about adoption addressed and would be ready to commit themselves to this option in a positive way.

Step two in Program B for those pursuing adoption would involve couples applying to adopt and going through a homestudy process. Various approaches to adoption homestudies have been tried across the country. One highly successful approach has been designed by Tressler Lutheran Social Services in York, Pennsylvania, and a curriculum guide for this model has been published by the North American Council on Adoptable Children as TEAM (Training and Education in Adoption Methods) Parent Preparation Handbook.) The Tressler Lutheran model prepares parents for special needs placements, but most of its elements are as appropriate for couples considering only infant adoption. The model encourages the use of parent/volunteers in the homestudy team. It allows preadoptive couples to take control of their study/education process. The approach involves a great deal of group work, with those involved increasingly exposed to and involved personally with one another as they come to know each other. In the end, couples do their own screening and decide for themselves if and when they are ready to adopt and what kind of limits they need to set for themselves on the particular needs of children they would consider. The program is highly structured and involves the use of a number of decision-making worksheets and discussion sessions facilitated by the adoption worker. In this particular model, once couples have decided to proceed with special needs adoption, they are encouraged to make use of the various states' exchange books to specifically pick out children in which they are interested. In this agency, which does not serve as a care provider for children, adoption workers serve as advocates within the system for prospective parents, assisting them in working as efficiently as possible through proper channels to achieve a placement and successfully working through the adoption process. The assumption of this model and others is that adoption-built families which include special needs children will need continuing services, some of which can be provided through the agency, and some of which can be provided through other agencies and/or parent groups. Thus adoptors are encouraged and expected to become families which consistently acknowledge adoption's differences and are highly involved from the beginning in parent groups.

Those couples who will be adopting infants need to spend their post-study/pre-placement time actively preparing for their coming child as a pregnant couple would. Couples should be referred to classes designed to deal with preparation for parenthood issues that are universal (such as infant care and feeding; selection of equipment, clothing and furniture; choosing a physician; parenting's impact upon family dynamics, etc.) as well as providing education and support in areas unique to adoption (i.e., preparing family and friends, dealing with the world at large, positive adoption language, resolving residual negative feelings about infertility, developing a sense of entitlement, etc.) In order to be optimally effective, such classes must be offered independent of an adoption agency through an objective source such as RESOLVE, a parent group, the Red Cross, hospital parent education programs, etc., and must mandatorily be taught by an adoptive parent with training in nursing, childbirth preparation, education, social work, counseling, or teaching. A successful model for such programs as they have been offered by Indiana RESOLVE is the 233 page curriculum guide *Our Child: Preparation For Parenting In Adoption — Instructor's Guide* by Carol A. Hallenbeck, B.S., R.N. (see resources).

No matter what adoption option preadoptive parents are planning to pursue, their education should center on their acquiring skills in acknowledging adoption's differences and developing a compassionate understanding of the wide variety of needs likely to be felt by those experiencing this process. Adoption today is changing at a rapid pace. Though it has been less frequently chosen by those dealing with an untimely pregnancy, it is occurring more frequently that children born to single mothers who are unsuccessful at their attempts to parent either voluntarily or involuntarily find their way into the system at an older and subsequently "less adoptable" age.

Some mental health and social work professionals feel that reestablishing professionally facilitated adoption as a positive option for dealing with an untimely pregnancy would save many children and their birthparents from the emotional scars of such an unsuccessful start. Such a reestablishment, however, is unlikely to happen if institutional adoption as we know it does not change. Change, however, can be frightening. It represents the possibility of the status quo going out of control rather than being improved. Thus, some of the newer approaches to adoption counseling being advocated by a variety of agencies and groups, approaches which advocate more openness and communication varying from anonymous one time letter exchanges to continuing communication and involvement between birth and adoptive families, are highly controversial.

Only the bravest —or in some cases the most desperate — of traditional adoptors have invited the concept of openness in adoption. Perhaps this is because adoption has been for so long a totally secretive institution. Open adoption has existed for a long time, however —in the black community, where adoptions historically have been informally arranged within extended families; in step-parent adoptions; in many placements of older children; in some private adoptions. Only in suggesting that it become part of the mainstream in adoption has it become so controversial.

The appeal of openness for birthparents lies in the possibility of personal reassurance that the child for whom they make such a plan is going to a loving family. Birthparents, too, feel a need for control in adoption. In making a decision not to parent a child to whom they have given birth —a decision that goes against current mainstream values in society —birthparents may feel that in having the opportunity to participate in the selection of their child's parents and to communicate directly with them about their reasons for choosing the adoption alternative and their hopes and dreams for themselves and their child they can deal more effectively with the long term effects of this loss.

Adoptive parents, too, often come to wish that they could have more information for their children about birthfamilies. Having participated in two traditional adoptions, my husband and I adopted a third time in an open situation. We would not have been ready for such direct communication before we had parented our first son —but, then, we had not been prepared for this possibility either. With our second adoption we had come to a place where we wished that we could have at least a letter exchange with our daughter's birthmother. We were told that she wasn't ready for this. We met our third child's birthmother. It was an emotional experience, but not in the least bit frightening. The exchange of information between us satisfied for each of us a hunger for knowledge of one another. The possibility of speaking to one another made each of real to the other, not the fantasized image we have of our other children's parents and they must have of us. In listening to her explain her decision and directly explain that our family was what she wanted for her child, our daughter's birthmother began the development of our sense of entitlement by expressing to us her confidence that we could raise her child as she wanted her raised. This woman is not the phantom "unknown woman" said to haunt some adoptive parents' fantasies. She is a real person who gave us the gift of her child and the knowledge that she felt her decision to be a good one.

Had we been better prepared, perhaps we would have wanted to meet our son's birthmother nine years ago. We know that we would like to meet her now. Perhaps if our first daughter's mother had been better prepared she would have allowed herself to communicate with us. Then again, perhaps she would not, perhaps we would not. Openness is one change that is part of the new directions in adoption. But it cannot be considered the only healthy option. Perhaps what damaged the old system more than anything else was a refusal to be flexible, to plan each adoption on the basis of the unique needs of two specific sets of parents and a particular child. Cooperative adoption will work well for some adoptors and birthparents, but it would not be appropriate for all. Those interested in examining cooperative adoption might find of interest Kathleen Silber and Phylis Speedlin's *Dear Birthmother* (Corona Publishing, 1982), Suzanne Arms' *To Love and Let Go* (Knopf, 1983), *Cooperative Adoption* by Sharon Kaplan and Mary Jo Rillera, and the pamphlet "The Birthparents' Perspective" which is available from Concerned United Birthparents of Dover, New Hampshire.

A word of caution about expectations of professionals other than adoption workers in serving adoption-built families. Increasingly, families are complaining about the lack of understanding of the dynamics unique to adoption displayed by their children's physicians, psychometrists, family counselors, mental health workers, teachers, etc. On the one hand parents complain that too often everything is blamed on the child's adoptive status, and on the other hand they find professionals unwilling to see adoption as different from any other method of family building. Perhaps adoption professionals are in the best position to breach this crisis of confidence if they can once bridge the gap between themselves and adoptors. Flexibility will be required to bridge this gap, just as it is vital to other changes necessary to improve the adoption system. As this book was going to press a study called *Concepts In Adoption* by Patricia L. Holmes was about to be released. *Concepts* was the result of a survey done with professionals and adoptors from across the U.S. in an effort to identify particular areas that are problematic in the relationship between adoptors and educators, adoptors and counselors, adoptors and medical professionals, adoptors and social workers, etc. Perhaps this study will provide us all as adoption advocates with materials for the work of change.

All of us involved in adoption have an important responsibility to the families created and separated by this process. In particular our responsibility lies with children who have been adopted. We best fulfill that responsibility when we keep it uppermost in our minds and remain open to change and to new ideas.

RESOURCES

Often large publishers are hesitant to accept adoption-related manuscripts because their appeal to a minority of the population makes them unlikely to become dollar generating best sellers. Consequently the limited number of adoption-related books that have been well promoted are often of three categories: "how-to" guides for those who wish to adopt, which quickly become outdated; sensationalistic first-person stories; saccarin-sweet first person stories. Much of the material that addresses issues of importance to those touched by adoption personally or professionally will be found in the titles introduced by smaller publishing houses, which are more issue-oriented than dollar-oriented, and in the booklets and newsletters and journals published by voluntary and professional groups with an adoption interest.

The resources below have been carefully selected and pared to a minimum so that the reader is likely to have time to peruse them all. Each group and each book will lead you to more materials on the same subject. Where books may be difficult to locate, suggested sources for ordering them have been included.

INFERTILITY

RESOLVE, INC. — a national organization offering education, referral, support, and advocacy services to infertile couples and professionals working with them through a network of chapters in over 50 cities nationwide. Chapters offer monthly meetings, periodic large educational programs, literature, telephone counseling, referral to medical help and to alternatives to infertility, formal support groups led by trained personnel and newsletters. Chapters are run by volunteers, primarily from offices in homes, and are supported by dues and tax deductible donations. The national office of RESOLVE (P.O. Box 474, Belmont, MA 02178, telephone 617-484-2424) can put you in touch with the chapter closest to you and/or the regional representative of the chapters in your area.

THE CENTER FOR COMMUNICATIONS IN INFERTILITY — attempts to serve as a clearinghouse for infertility related information for lay persons and professionals. Towards this end the Center publishes the bi-monthly magazine *Perspectives On Infertility,* featuring articles on medical, surgical, and pharmaceutical advances in the area of infertility as well as the emotional aspects of the problem. Contributors to this magazine directed to a lay audience are medical specialists and mental health professionals. Information on membership in the CENTER, which includes a subscription to the magazine, may be obtained by writing to them at P.O. Box 516, Yorktown Heights, NY 10598.

THE AMERICAN FERTILITY SOCIETY, 1609 13th Avenue South, Suite 101, Birmingham, AL 35256, is a highly respected professional organization for physicians with an interest in the medical treatment of infertility. A list of members by state is available to those in search of a physician, and the organization publishes a number of materials on infertility for both lay and professional audiences.

Stepping Stones is a Christian focused newsletter for infertile couples published every other month by the Stepping Stones Ministry, P.O. Box 11141, Wichita, KS 67211 as a not-for-profit ministry of Central Christian Church in Wichita. While no subscription fee is charged, tax deductible donations to the program are welcomed.

Young Couples International is a fertility/infertility newsletter published six times a year. For information about subscribing write 216 Calhoun St., Charleston, SC 29401.

Each year new books are published which address the medical issues and advances in infertility. Because infertility is such a rapidly changing field of medicine, these books become quickly outdated. For the newest and most highly recommended books and fact sheets in this area, contact RESOLVE. The books below address the emotional aspects of infertility —a topic less frequently considered in the literature.

Johnston, Patricia Irwin, **Understanding: A Guide to Impaired Fertility For Family and Friends** (Perspectives Press, 1983) —a 28 page booklet designed to be read by those close to an infertile couple as well as by the couple themselves and professionals working with them to familiarize these caring others with the emotional side effects of a fertility impairment and to offer ways that family and friends can offer help and avoid aggravating the problem. Order through the publisher, Perspectives Press, 905 West Wildwood Ave., Dept. A., Fort Wayne, IN 46807 at $ 3.50.

Menning, Barbara Eck; **Infertility: A Guide for the Childless Couple** (Prentice Hall, 1977) is the soon-to-become-classic first book to address the psycho-social impact of infertility at all. This is a must read for anyone interested in infertility at any level, though the medical section is some what out of date. It is still available in some book stores and is always available through RESOLVE, of which Ms. Menning was the founder and first executive director.

Stigger, Judith A.; **Coping With Infertility** (Augsburg Publishing House, 1983) Particularly valuable about this slim paperback are its discussion of spirituality and religion in the decision making process of infertility, as well as good advice on choosing a doctor, evaluating alternatives, etc. If you have difficulty finding this book in local book stores, order from Indiana RESOLVE, Inc., 218 S. Liberty, Dept. F, Bluffton, IN 46714 at $5.70.

ORGANIZATIONS WITH AN ADOPTION-RELATED FOCUS

The following groups have been carefully selected from among hundreds across the country with an interest in adoption because they each have a special perspectives on the subject that may provide valuable insights for you. Each publishes a newsletter and has available other written materials. When you are writing to inquire about their services, please include a long self-addressed stamped envelope for the use of these not-for-profit organizations in replying.

ADOPTEES LIBERTY MOVEMENT ASSOCIATION (ALMA) was the first organization formed to assist adoptees in connecting with their birthfamilies. Chapters all over the country may be reached through the national office at P.O. Box 154, Washington Bridge Station, New York, NY 10033.

AMERICAN ADOPTION CONGRESS is an umbrella group for the hundreds of search groups across the country. Annually it holds a national convention with a variety of speakers on topics of interest to those fighting for adoption reform. Write to the AAC at Box 44040, L'Enfant Plaza, Washington DC 20026-0040.

CHILD WELFARE LEAGUE OF AMERICA is a professional organization of child placing agencies which deals not just with adoption, but with foster care, juvenile justice, and many other topics relating to the needs of children. Their national office at at 67 Irving Place, New York, NY 10003.

CONCERNED UNITED BIRTHPARENTS (CUB) offers support and advocacy services to those who have relinquished a child for adoption and lobbies for reform of adoption laws and policies. The national office at 595 Central Ave., Dover, NH 03820 can put you in touch with branches across the country and provide you with a list of their publications.

FAMILIES ADOPTING CHILDREN EVERYWHERE (FACE) is a support, referral, and education service for families built by adoption, with particular emphasis on foreign adoptions and special needs adoptions. Based in Maryland, this progressive organization's newsletter alone makes membership valuable to people from all over the country. P.O. Box 28058, Northwood Station, Baltimore, MD 21239.

LATIN AMERICAN PARENTS ASSOCIATION (LAPA) is a multi-chapter organization focusing on the needs of children from Latin America by assisting in parent initiated adoptions, sending material assistance to Latin American orphanages, and offering opportunities for families with Latin American children to support one another. Reach them at P.O. Box 72, Seaford, NY 11783.

NATIONAL COMMITTEE FOR ADOPTION, 1346 Connecticut Ave., NW,Suite 326, Washington DC 20036, is a membership organization of non-public child placement agencies, social work professionals, and adoptive parents working to enhance the image of adoption as a positive option in dealing with a problem pregnancy. NCFA focuses entirely upon positive adoption advocacy, working through states to pass legislation supportive of adoption. NCFA supports voluntary adoption registries rather than unrestricted open records and is concerned about lack of services and the possibilities for victimization for persons involved in a private adoption.

NORTH AMERICAN COUNCIL ON ADOPTABLE CHILDREN focuses on the importance of families for uprooted children by providing leadership and linkage among adoptive parent organizations in the United States and Canada. A network of volunteer state coordinators helps to link groups locally and nationally. The national office is located at 413 Duck Street, Alexandria, VA 22314.

OURS (Organization for United Response), INC. is a national organization with many chapters offering assistance, support, and advocacy for people who have become a family through adoption. Their bi-monthly magazine is a must for adoption-built families. Contact OURS at 3307 Hwy. 100 N., Suite 203, Minneapolis, MN 55422.

PARENTS FOR PRIVATE ADOPTION is a fledgling group of families who support independent or non-agency adoption as a viable method of family planning. To this end they work for political and social reforms in the adoption scene, advocating for birthparents, educating the public and potential adoptors about adoption alternatives including open adoption, and conducting a research project on private adoption. Contact PPA at P.O. Box 7, Pawlet, VT 05761.

POST ADOPTION CENTER FOR RESEARCH AND EDUCATION (PACER), 477-15th St., Rm. 200, Oakland, CA 94612, serves all members of the adoption triad through support groups and education. Two publications of this group, **Dialogue For Understanding I and II,** can be helpful to those interested in expanding their personal perspectives.

SPECIAL READING

Following are some reading materials with specialized focuses. Several of them have been mentioned earlier in the text.

Dukette, Rita. **"Value Issues in Present-Day Adoption."** *Child Welfare* (63) May-June, 1984, pp. 233 - 244.

Fiegelman, William and Arnold R. Silverman; *Chosen Children: New Patterns of Adoptive Relationships* (1983) — reports on a study by two State University of New

York sociologists of several hundred adoptive families, including traditional infertile adoptors and fertile preferential adoptors, adoptees who arrived as infants and those who were older children, American and foreign placements, same race and transracial, attempting to draw inferences about what factors predict positive and negative outcomes in adoption. Praeger Publishers, CBS Educational and Professional Publishing, 521 Fifth Ave., New York, NY 10175, $24.95.

Holmes, Patricia L.; **Concepts In Adoption** (1984) — a report of a survey of the conflicting concepts of adoptive parents, teachers, doctors, counselors, psychologists, psychiatrists and other professionals concerning adoption. Issues addressed include awareness of children's needs and adoption dynamics, identity and self esteem, problem ownership, etc. Order through Richlynn Publications, P.O. Box 1488, Dept. P, Gig Harbor, WA 98335, $ 7.95.

Holmes, Patricia L.; **Supporting An Adoption** (1982) — a booklet designed for family members, neighbors, friends, clergy, etc. of a family expanding by adoption which offers numerous explanations of the adoption process and ways in which caring others can either support or unwittingly undermine the growing family. Another Richlynn Publication (see above), $ 3.10.

Johnston, Patricia Irwin; **Perspectives On A Grafted Tree** (1983) — a collection of poems written by birthparents, adoptees, adoptive parents and extended family members expressing the wide variety of feelings both positive and negative which are part of the gains and losses, happiness and pain felt by all of those touched by adoption. Perspectives Press, 905 West Wildwood Ave., Dept. A., Fort Wayne, Indiana 46807, $14.20.

Kirk, H. David; **Adoptive Kinship: A Modern Institution In Need of Reform** (1981) — an expansion of the

Shared Fate theory of adoptive kinship introduced in Kirk's classic *Shared Fate,* Butterworths, Toronto.

Kirk, H. David; **Shared Fate** (updated version, 1984) — the sociological theory that adoption built families share role handicaps that can become positive tools for establishing strong, trusting family relationships was first introduced in this book of the early 1960's recently rereleased by Butterworth's of Toronto.

Koch, Janice; **Our Baby: A Birth and Adoption Story** (1985) — what makes this small book for very young children special is that it is the only book currently available which introduces sex education and reproduction to the child who was adopted. Perspectives Press, 905 West Wildwood Ave., Dept. A., Fort Wayne, IN 46807, $ 6.20 paperback, $11.20 hardcover.

Smith, Jerome and Franklin I. Miroff; **You're Our Child: A Social/Psychological Approach to Adoption** (University Press of America, 1981) — a book introducing adoptive parents and prospective adoptors to the tasks unique to traditional adoptors in building a sense of entitlement to their children and thus a successful family. Order through Indiana RESOLVE, Inc., 218 South Liberty, Dept. F, Bluffton, IN 46714, $ 9.00.

Spencer, Marietta; **Understanding Adoption as a Family Building Option** (1980) — this booklet from the multimedia series *Understanding Adoption: Resources and Activities for Teaching Adults About Adoption* includes an excellent discussion of positive adoption language. Order at $ 1.95 per copy from the publisher, Social Science Education Consortium, 855 Broadway, Boulder, CO 80202.

PARENT PREPARATION MATERIALS

The Baby Decision by Merle Bombardieri (Rawson-Wade, 1981). A step by step guide to making the decision of whether or not to become a parent —for the first time or as a repeat. The author offers decision-making workshops to couples throughout the country using this book as her premise. Order through Growth Marks, P.O. Box 246, West Roxbury, MA 02132 at $ 9.95.

Family Building Thru Adoption — the course outline for a series of classes in adoption decision making offered by the volunteers from Families Adopting Children Everywhere. Order from FACE, P.O. Box 28058, Northwood Station, Baltimore, MD 21239, at $ 7.00.

Guidelines for Organizing and Teaching Adoptive Parent Classes by Beth Lockhart. P.O. Box 32114, Phoenix, AZ 85064.

Our Child: Preparation For Parenting In Adoption — Instructor's Guide by Carol A. Hallenbeck, R.N., B.S. (1984) — a step by step curriculum guide for offering a series of four classes in parent preparation for those who will be adopting infants, including an extensive bibliography and resource list of free and inexpensive materials, a guide to audio visual resources, etc. Order at $20.20 from Our Child Press, 800 Maple Glen Lane, Drawer 3A, Wayne, PA 19087.

INFORMATION ON OPEN ADOPTION

Lutheran Social Services of Texas, 615 Elm St., San Antonio, TX 78202.

Sunny Ridge Family Center, 2 South 426 Orchard Rd., Wheaton, IL 60187.

The OPT Program of WACAP, P.O. Box 2009, Port Angeles, WA 98362.

Concerned United Birthparents (see address above). Order the booklets "Understanding the Birthparent" ($5) and "Birthparents' Perspective" ($1).

Arms, Suzanne, **To Love and Let Go** (Alfred A. Knopf, 1983). A series of case studies of several women who chose various forms of open adoption in planning for their children and of the couples who adopted these children. $14.95.

Kaplan, Sharon and Mary Jo Rillera; **Cooperative Adoption A Handbook** (Tri-Adoption Library, 1983). A handbook designed for use in decision making concerning openness in adoption by both birthparents and adoptive parents. Common questions are included and answered, as are sample documents, guidelines for setting parameters, and suggestions for finding appropriate partners for such an adoption. Order from Tri-Adoption Library, P.O. Box 638, Westminster, CA 92683, $14.95.

Panor, Reuben and Annette Baran. **"Open Adoption as Standard Practice."** **Child Welvare** (63) May-June, 1984, pp. 245 - 250.

Silber, Kathleen and Phylis Speedlin; **Dear Birthmother** (Corona Publishing, 1983). A discussion of the open adoption services of Lutheran Social Services of San Antonio featuring a collection of letters written between birth and adoptive parents. $ 7.95.

INDEX

LET US INTRODUCE OURSELVES . . .

Perspectives Press is a narrowly focused publishing company. The materials we produce or distribute all speak to issues related to infertility or to adoption. Our purpose is to promote understanding of these issues and to educate and sensitize those personally experiencing these life situations, professionals who work in infertility and adoption, and the public at large. Perspectives Press titles are never duplicative. We seek out and publish materials that are currently unavailable through traditional sources.

Our authors have special credentials: they are people whose personal and professional lives provide an interwoven pattern for what they write. If you are writing about infertility or adoption, we invite you to contact us with a query letter so that we can determine whether your materials fit into our publishing scheme.

905 W. Wildwood Avenue
Fort Wayne, Indiana 46807

Books Available from Perspectives Press

Perspectives on a Grafted Tree

An Adoptor's Advocate

Understanding: A Guide to Impaired Fertility for Family and Friends

Our Baby: A Birth and Adoption Story

Our Child: Preparation for Parenting in Adoption

Everything You Ever Wanted to Know about Planning an Adoption Special Event

And coming in the spring of 1986 . . . *The Mulberry Bird: Story of an Adoption*

Perspectives Press . . . the infertility
and adoption publishers.

DATE DUE

5/3,90			
5/17/90			
JAN 2 1992			
JUN 5 - 1992			
SEP 29 1992			
DEC 21 1992			
~~JUN 23~~			
SEP 2 4 1998			
NOV 2 1 2001			
MAY 3 0 2002			